ALL IT TAKES IS *ONE*

DROP YOUR ONE **BIG** HIDDEN BELIEF & MASTER YOUR LIFE

by

Ray Doktor, Psy. D.

Copyright ©2024
ALL IT TAKES IS ONE
Drop Your One BIG Hidden Belief & Master Your Life
by
Ray Doktor, Psy. D.

All rights reserved. No part of this publication may be reproduced, distributed, or transmitted in any form or by any means, including photocopying, recording, or other electronic or mechanical methods, without the prior written permission of the publisher, except in the case of brief quotations embodied in critical reviews and certain other noncommercial uses permitted by copyright law.

For permission requests, write to the publisher, addressed "Attention: Permissions Coordinator,"
carol@markvictorhansenlibrary.com

Quantity sales special discounts are available on quantity purchases by corporations, associations, and others. For details, contact the publisher at carol@markvictorhansenlibrary.com

Orders by U.S. trade bookstores and wholesalers.
Email: carol@markvictorhansenlibrary.com

Illustrations by Jesper Juul Habraken
Cover Design & Book Layout - DBree, StoneBear Design

Manufactured and printed in the United States of America distributed globally by markvictorhansenlibrary.com
New York | Los Angeles | London | Sydney

ISBN: 979-8-88581-154-5 Hardback
ISBN: 979-8-88581-155-2 Paperback
ISBN: 979-8-88581-156-9 eBook
Library of Congress Control Number: 2024904947

DEDICATION

I'm uncertain how other authors feel about dedicating books to special individuals; for me, it has presented a challenge, as numerous people have been integral to my journey and growth. It is not my intent to elevate one above another, for each has uniquely contributed to my life and the open heart from which this book flows.

In dedicating this book, I am mindful not to exclude anyone or to place undue importance on one person over another. This work and the teachings I impart, which continue to evolve, are a mirror of my growing consciousness and open heart. My life has been like a train journey, where passengers come and go—some stay for the long ride, while others depart swiftly. Whether it was a brief conversation that expanded my perspective or a lasting friendship, I have been fortunate to encounter many beautiful souls who have contributed to this book's creation. To all, I offer my love and gratitude, whether or not our paths cross again.

I have been blessed with a tremendously supportive family, particularly my parents. Raised in poverty during the Great Depression, they endeavored to give my brothers and me everything they lacked in their own childhood. Their generosity extended beyond material goods, like essential items and electric guitars that supported our hobbies, to our education. They were always just a phone call away, ready to engage in genuine, transparent conversations. The essence of my values—work ethic, integrity, and the aspiration to be a good human being contributing to the community—stemmed from the core of my parents' essence. Robert and Michiko, my parents, were pioneers in their generosity—always willing to donate, lend a helping hand, and support the underprivileged. They embraced inclusivity across all ethnicities and races, accepted people of all sexual orientations, and even celebrated my personal expression, which in the '80s meant wearing eyeliner, earrings, and dyeing my hair.

My life's current richness owes much to the steadfast support of my friend Amy, the godmother of my son, Maximus. Amy has been an unwavering motherly and friendly presence for him and a person who has invested tremendous energy into our lives, even when facing her own challenges. Her devoted love for our family has enabled me to leave the city and write this book, all while raising Maximus amidst the beauty of mountains, forests, running streams, and a vibrant artistic and spiritual community.

Dr. Morris Netherton profoundly influenced my life through his teachings and his cautionary advice: "Ray, don't become like me." He had a habit of overworking and neglecting self-care. Unbeknownst to me, he had passed away, but he communicated his transition to the other side through a dream. The insights I continue to receive from him and other masters are a testament to his enduring legacy.

My son Maximus stands as my greatest teacher. His unconditional love is unparalleled; it has transformed not just my understanding but my heart. Prior to his arrival, my teachings were more intellectual than emotional. Yet, witnessing his innocent, joyous gaze—reflecting back my own imperfections—has been profoundly humbling. In moments of impatience, his serene presence, so reminiscent of a wise little Buddha, reminds me to remain present, curious, and open-hearted. Maximus, in his innate wisdom, remains unaffected by the haste of the world, a lesson in itself.

Maximus, you embody the person I aspire to be, seeing the world's beauty through an unclouded lens. If we all viewed the world as an innocent child does, with unjudging eyes and a pure heart, harm would be a stranger to us. Compassion, after all, is innate when we embrace the world with the heart of a child at play.

Acknowledging my humanity, I anticipate that upon the book's

Dedication

release, I might reflect on what could have been included, recognizing that I am still mastering the art of relinquishing perfection and appreciating the beauty within the process. "Space Oddity," crafted by David Bowie in 1969—the year of my birth—is to me a timeless classic. Its creation, I imagine, was an act of releasing his art into the universe without knowing the profound impact it would have on his career or the profound connection it would make with listeners. In this same spirit, I offer my gratitude to God, the Source, the Universe, the Great Spirit, for the privilege to convey art, stir emotions, and share the narrative of my life through this book.

INTRODUCTION

What if I told you that the master key to the life you truly desire lies in your hidden beliefs? What if I told you that you only really have one or two BIG hidden beliefs that are holding you back in your life? What if I told you that letting go of these hidden beliefs from your mind and body would instantly have a profound positive impact on your life? Finally, what if I could show you exactly how to do this in as little time as possible, just like I have for thousands of others like you? If this resonates with you, then this book is written for you!

If you're exploring self-development for the first time, it's normal to feel hesitant. You may wonder if this book is the right choice, if there are better alternatives, or if you're on the correct path. It's also common to be curious about the author—that's me—and whether I truly live by the principles I share. I respect your critical thinking and openness; they show your commitment to finding a path that feels right for you. This book advocates for personal responsibility, and I commend your diligence.

While reading this book, you may find yourself challenged by my perspectives, especially if they clash with your existing beliefs. Although I offer new, positive viewpoints to support you and encourage a shift in mindset, change can provoke strong emotions and push you out of your comfort zone. This response is typical when confronting fears, facing the unknown, and struggling to let go of control, particularly of beliefs we cling to simply because they are familiar. It's important to approach this process with patience. You might also consider sharing the reading and exercises with a trusted friend.

This book is intentionally structured to provide a clear understanding of how I tackle negative hidden beliefs and emotions, as well as their

Introduction

origins. Each chapter builds on the previous one, offering practical tools for immediate use. These tools aim to enhance your well-being, improve your relationships, increase your confidence, enable you to express yourself more authentically, foster greater self-trust, and cultivate a more positive view of life.

And if you're experienced in the healing arts but still find yourself wrestling with issues, despite understanding the influences of your triggers, this book may assist you. You might still be engaging in self-sabotage or experiencing relationship troubles, even with your wealth of knowledge and experience. This book aims to help you finally conquer these challenges, solidifying the best version of yourself and the self-love you've been consistently striving for.

We all have origin stories that we believe mark the beginning, filled with struggles against the demons of negative thoughts, feelings, and ongoing challenges. My own journey to self-love, acceptance, and recognizing my worth began with numerous early childhood challenges. I suffered from asthma and severe allergies, which meant my life revolved around allergy shots and countless pills. These medications made me hyperactive and greatly hindered my ability to concentrate and focus on schoolwork. During guitar lessons, I couldn't retain information and had to learn through sensation and sound. Today, I might have been diagnosed with dyslexia or a similar learning disorder.

I was born with tibial torsion, a condition that made my feet turn inward. Learning to walk was a challenge, and I wore leg braces similar to those worn by the character Forrest Gump in the 1994 movie until I was six. Other kids mocked me, labeling me as a gimp or cripple. However, much like Forrest Gump, when the braces came off, I discovered I could run incredibly fast. I even won several races, including one notably named "The Fastest Feet in the West." This advantage in speed as a child boosted my self-esteem in sports and races. Despite this, I still struggled with self-worth issues.

Growing up as a half-Asian, Jewish, Buddhist boy was quite different from the white conservative Christians I attended school with. I faced racism and bullying because of my religion and ethnicity. Stress from home and side effects from my medication led me to develop an anxiety disorder known as trichotillomania, which made me pull out my own hair. I had bald spots and was teased for this as well. It felt as if life was conspiring against me, forcing me to overcome awkwardness at a young age.

When I reached the fourth grade, my peers began to accept me because I was funny and fearless. They gave me the nickname "Crazy Ray," which is even noted in my elementary school yearbook. I often pushed boundaries and used shock value to gain attention and popularity, like acting as a clown or even driving my parents' car to pick up friends when I was just 12. But acting like a wild child never truly satisfied me, as I was doing these things for attention, not because they reflected my authentic self.

During my adolescent years, my ego took a significant hit when I became the star running back for my junior high football team, only to break and fracture my ankle and fibula before the season began. Walking on crutches for three months, I felt overlooked as I couldn't score touchdowns to gain positive attention. This situation plunged me into deep depression.

However, my reading and writing teacher, Mrs. Jenkins, whom I didn't particularly like, and the feeling seemed mutual, sparked a change in me by saying, "Stop feeling sorry for yourself!" On Friday, December 16th, 1983, the last day before Christmas vacation, I decided to drastically alter my image. I started wearing black leather pants, punk-style shirts and accessories; I dyed my hair and wore makeup to school. As I strolled through the school hallways, I can still recall the stares of all my classmates. I was dressed as a completely different

Introduction

person than I had been before.

It felt similar to David Bowie's alter ego, Ziggy Stardust. The old Ray Doktor, who wallowed in self-pity, vanished that day. I started a few punk bands, got a tattoo at 15, and mingled with older people in the Los Angeles and Orange County punk scene, including Mike Ness from Social Distortion. Even though I still didn't fully love myself, this new persona served as a temporary band-aid, helping me to receive positive attention.

When I was sixteen, I overdosed on PCP (Phencyclidine), leading to my second near-death experience. The first happened when I was six, falling three stories from an under-construction building with loose scaffolding. At the time, I didn't realize that these experiences had gifted me two crucial lessons: the absence of fear of death and a strong belief in God, seeing us as humans on a spiritual journey. Experiencing the fifth-dimensional reality (spirit) through a near-death situation changed my perspective on life and physical reality.

Even though I had witnessed and experienced the spiritual realm, I remained unhappy, making poor choices, and living recklessly. After getting arrested for a DUI (driving under the influence) in my early twenties, I was mandated to attend therapy. This marked the beginning of my healing journey. While touring as a dancer, I met a woman named Marci who gifted me the book *You Can Heal Your Life* by Louise Hay.

Louise Hay's teachings resonated with me deeply, as though they were reminding me of my true self and potential. I developed a fascination with metaphysics, psychology, epigenetics, shamanism, mysticism, religion, and anything that could help me feel like an empowered human being. I became a dedicated seeker of happiness and truth, devouring numerous self-help books, attending spiritual growth events and retreats, and consulting with healers.

While searching for an office space to transform into a recording

Introduction

studio for my music career, I met Dr. Morris Netherton in Pasadena, California. We formed an instant connection and developed a bond like that of a father and son. Although he had retired from teaching and mentoring, my enthusiasm rekindled his passion for instruction, and I became his apprentice. Together, we traveled the world to train various professionals, including psychotherapists, psychologists, counselors, coaches, and self-development practitioners.

We taught them in his process and technique known as "The Netherton Method," which was inspired by his colleagues Fritz Perls, Carl Rogers, and Dr. Stanislav Grof. This method drew a diverse array of students from the healing arts, including Richard Bandler and John Grinder, who were Tony Robbins' teachers and the founders of Neuro-Linguistic Programming (NLP). During my mentorship, I continued my education, returning to school to earn an undergraduate degree in human behavior, a master's degree in counseling psychology, and a doctoral degree in clinical psychology.

Drawing on a diverse range of experiences, including healing from childhood trauma, navigating intimate relationships, embracing fatherhood, undergoing clinical training, and studying under various masters, I have developed my unique coaching methods and philosophies. This book represents my three decades of experience as a life coach, the invaluable lessons I've gained from my mentors, as well as my triumphs and challenges. I'm excited to share these insights with you in this book.

Thank you for allowing me to be a part of your extraordinary journey towards healing and wholeness. This book is not just a guide; it is a companion as you navigate the complexities of self-growth and discovery. I honor your willingness to embrace change, to face the depths of your being, and to emerge empowered and renewed. Here, trust can flourish, and every step, however tentative, becomes a dance with possibility. This path is not always easy, but it is infinitely

Introduction

rewarding. As you turn each page and delve into the work, know that you are not alone—I am with you, cheering you on, celebrating every victory, no matter how small it may seem.

With warmth and gratitude,

Ray Doktor, Psy. D.

TABLE OF CONTENTS

Chapter 1
The Courage to Begin: A Step into the Unknown 1

Chapter 2
Beyond Invisible Walls: Escaping the
Psychological Prison 14

Chapter 3
Mental Blueprint: Decoding the Structures of Belief 34

Chapter 4
The Illusion of Safety: Revealing Hidden Benefits 54

Chapter 5
Claiming Individual Power: Breaking Free
from the Collective Script 67

Chapter 6
Rising Above Myths: Unleashing the Inner Hero 74

Chapter 7:
Vital Vortexes: Activating Your Energy Anatomy 94

Chapter 8
Ascending Beyond Blame: Claiming
Personal Sovereignty 113

Chapter 9
The Shadow Dance: Navigating Personality Friction 126

Chapter 10
Illuminated Paths: Steering Through the Continuum
of Self-Healing 138

Chapter 11
Beyond the Matrix: The Emergence of the
Heart-Centered Human 157

About the Author 167

1
The Courage to Begin: A Step into the Unknown

Mary sought my coaching due to her anxiety in new social environments and around large crowds. On the day of her initial appointment, she called me from her car parked outside my building, expressing her apprehension and proposing a reschedule. I softly reminded her that this was the exact issue she wanted to address. Conceding to my point, she agreed to a meeting in the park across from my office.

There, I guided Mary through a tree grounding exercise. With her back against the tree, she closed her eyes and focused on her breathing. As she inhaled, I had her imagine bringing down heaven's energy through her body and into the earth through her feet. Then, on the exhale, I had her imagine taking in earth energy up through her feet and into the crown of her head. With each breath, she became more grounded and centered.

In roughly ten minutes, Mary opened her eyes. She appeared radiant and calm, ready to continue our session in my office. Here, she dove deeper into her survival mechanisms, sharing that her anxiety had heightened after beginning a new job. She also disclosed past traumas, such as bullying, date rape, and sexual harassment. This conversation enlightened her about her fear of change and initiating new endeavors.

Unfortunately, some individuals become emotionally stuck and fail to attend their first self-development retreat or coaching session.

1. The Courage to Begin: A Step Into the Unknown

They leave self-improvement workshops and coaching sessions overwhelmed by fear. Despite having hope and knowing something positive could change, hidden traumas and beliefs become like huge cracks in the sidewalk, deterring us on our walk towards healing.

Meredith's Resistance to Feedback

Meredith and Jack shared that their marriage was on the rocks. Meredith claimed that Jack avoids conversations, and she didn't trust him. Jack, on the other hand, said that Meredith gets defensive when he shares his feelings, which is why he avoids having conversations with her.

In our session, Jack bravely shared his genuine feelings. Yet, Meredith swiftly dismissed his emotions rather than offering empathy. I suggested that she try to understand Jack's viewpoint and the reasons for his feelings, whether or not she agreed with him. However, Meredith reacted defensively to my feedback.

I validated Meredith's feelings, despite her seeming resistance to Jack's emotions. I invited her to investigate her own emotions by closing her eyes and identifying where in her body she felt them. After a moment of introspection, Meredith grew emotional and confessed that her father, a narcissist, had consistently criticized her, leading her to believe she could never do anything right.

I encouraged Meredith to identify any link between her current feelings and the childhood experiences she'd just shared in our coaching session. She admitted that she felt as though I was pointing out her flaws and taking Jack's side. Encouraging her to reconsider Jack's attempts to express his feelings, she began to understand that she may have perceived his feedback as criticism emphasizing her shortcomings.

Using guided imagery, I guided Meredith towards the energy of her smiling children to help soften her heart. I then asked Jack to share

1. The Courage to Begin: A Step Into the Unknown

with Meredith why he shares his feelings, including feedback, with her. Jack gasped and said, "Meredith, you're my soulmate! I want to be with you forever. You're an extraordinary mother. I'm just trying to express myself, offer help, and just talk to you."

While Meredith sobbed, I asked her, "What would your relationship be like if your heart felt love when Jack shared his feelings with you?" After a lengthy pause, she responded, "Jack, I love you. I apologize for having been so defensive." They hugged, embracing each other with newfound understanding and compassion.

Dale and His Tendencies Towards People-Pleasing and Avoidance

Dale, a man in his late 40s, favored being single and engaging in casual relationships, which led him to avoid many social interactions. Despite his preference for remaining single, he felt a deep yearning for connection and was grappling with loneliness. Recognizing this, he knew change was necessary.

In our initial session, Dale seemed anxious and defensive, as if expecting judgment. He expressed dissatisfaction with traditional therapy, which led him to seek coaching. He had ended sessions with two previous therapists, feeling they were controlling and judgmental. Despite my empathetic approach, his discomfort persisted.

In our second session, Dale became fidgety and started sweating, indicating his wish to leave. I offered him the options to take a break or step outside. Despite his initial resistance, I managed to help him relax a bit. I asked if the feelings he was experiencing during our coaching sessions were similar to those he had with his previous therapists, to which he agreed. Upon asking if these feelings mirrored those in his relationship with his parents—where he felt both an obligation to speak to them and a sense of being controlled—he expressed surprise but confirmed this as well.

My intention was for Dale to examine his emotions and thoughts objectively and identify potential links between his experiences with his parents, past therapists, his projections, and our coaching sessions. I hoped to impart these insights even if he decided not to return for a follow-up. However, when Dale decided to leave, I respected his decision, saying, "I understand, Dale. You know what's best for you."

Dale scheduled another meeting three days later. Evidently, our previous session had sparked a cathartic experience for him. He confessed, "I felt uncomfortable and didn't want to upset you, feeling obliged to stay. But then you let me leave without stopping me. Was that a trick, Doc?" In response, I asked Dale how it felt to choose what he felt was best for him without worrying about my feelings. His main concern, he revealed, was not to upset me. I then asked Dale if he was afraid to be authentic and express his true thoughts, particularly in relationships where he didn't want to disappoint the other person. He emphatically replied, "Yes!"

This led to a transparent conversation about why Dale felt controlled by others because he was afraid to say "no" without feeling guilty. He had people-pleasing tendencies and never learned to establish boundaries, including with his parents, so he avoided people altogether. Dale began to realize that he wasn't responsible for others' happiness, especially if they were unhappy with his clear boundaries. He understood the need to become more comfortable expressing his authentic self and needs in a relationship. He recognized that his initial urge to abandon the coaching process was to avoid upsetting me. By feeling safe enough to express what he was feeling and thinking in real time within our coaching space, Dale made it part of his process to push through discomfort towards healing and transformation.

The Defensive and Protective Primal Brain

It's not uncommon for us, myself included, to abandon books,

1. The Courage to Begin: A Step Into the Unknown

coaches, or seminars, only to find value in them later on. In shadow work, we uncover hidden beliefs. These latent fears often intensify within a coaching container.

You may encounter confusion, negative thoughts, and uncomfortable emotions. Some suggestions or processes may even trigger you. However, don't hastily dismiss this book as *not for you* because of these obstacles. Defensiveness is a common response. A fresh perspective might make us feel wrong because it highlights areas where we need to grow. Yet, it's through such realizations that transformation occurs.

On this transformative journey, the relationships you cultivate with coaches, healers, fellow retreat participants, and supportive friends can mirror your growth, whether in healing past traumas or navigating current crises. As you become more self-aware, release outdated mindsets, and identify recurring patterns in your relationships, your consciousness expands. You may start to see how your current relationships reflect your unhealed parts and hint at your true potential.

During healing, people often struggle with uncertainty and apprehension. Questions like "Should I break up with my boyfriend now?" or "Should I quit my job to heal?" typically arise from a place of crisis or reaction, often surfacing even before our first coaching session. The challenge is discerning the right time for significant life changes. My guidance remains consistent: refrain from making hasty decisions unless you're facing immediate danger or harm. It's crucial to wait until you are in a state of calm and clarity. Decision-making should be rooted in personal growth and awareness, not just an escape from discomfort. Continually dodging conflict and failing to take personal responsibility can perpetuate the very cycle of drama you seek to overcome in your life. Decisions should be made from a place of personal growth and awareness, not merely as an escape from pain. Constantly avoiding conflict and not taking personal responsibility to confront your issues may be at the heart of perpetuating the cycle of drama in your life.

Many of us unknowingly adopt protective behaviors to avoid pain. While these survival mechanisms are crucial for our well-being, they can hinder our growth and openness to new experiences. They can also impose unnecessary urgency and time constraints on our healing process. We certainly don't want our primal survival instincts dictating our decisions, particularly when we're attempting to calm ourselves, gain insight, and break out of cyclical patterns. As Albert Einstein noted, doing the same thing repeatedly and expecting different results is unproductive.

The lower-path brain, known as the limbic system, consists of deep-brain structures such as the amygdala, hippocampus, and hypothalamus. It controls basic emotions, survival instincts, and routine behaviors, while also managing vital functions like heart rate and body temperature. In times of prolonged stress, it triggers the fight-or-flight response. While essential for survival and regulating functions like breathing, heart rate, and organ activity, the limbic system is not ideal for making choices about relationships, life decisions, or goals.

Conversely, the higher-path brain, or prefrontal cortex, located behind the forehead, manages reasoning, emotional regulation, problem-solving, planning, self-awareness, empathy, and perspective-taking. This brain region allows us to logically evaluate situations, leading to informed and healthier decisions. It is typically active when we feel safe or when we experience feelings of control, love, and compassion. This state enables us to interpret situations more objectively and calmly, making wise decisions from a place of clarity, confidence, and an elevated perspective. This could be as straightforward as taking a nap before addressing a stressful situation or re-evaluating a previously triggering message with a positive interpretation, recognizing that initial stress may have affected the initial perception.

1. The Courage to Begin: A Step Into the Unknown

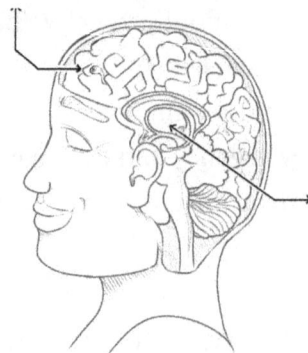

Long-term neglect or childhood trauma like sexual abuse can result in a hyper-vigilant nervous system. This can disrupt rational thinking in new relationships, opportunities, and situations, even without clear danger. Our perspectives on life and relationships, influenced by upbringing, culture, and childhood messages, may be difficult to challenge, particularly when they involve loved ones. The fear of losing their acceptance could stop us from questioning these ingrained beliefs. Additionally, repeated negative experiences, such as dating alcoholics, attracting narcissists, or constant business failures, can lead to limiting beliefs like "This is just my karma" or "I'm not good enough." Such past failures can spark a fear of trying new things, including self-development, keeping us anchored to familiar but unhelpful patterns.

The good news is that through conscious awareness and intention, we can regain control and transform negative thinking into positive and expansive feelings, thoughts, and actions once we soothe our nervous system. By cultivating new awareness, improving emotional control, and releasing unresolved beliefs and patterns, we can rewrite our old mental scripts and transform negative behaviors and emotions into healthier ones.

Optimal Methods for Benefiting from the Exercises and Processes in This Book

The exercises in this book are flexible and can be tailored to your preferences. While it's beneficial to try them all, focus on the ones that resonate with you and practice them as often as you like. You can integrate these exercises into your daily routine for grounding, stress relief, or to enhance joy. Use them as necessary, or simply for pleasure.

Perform the exercises when you have uninterrupted time in a quiet, distraction-free environment, whether indoors or outdoors. Allow your nervous system to relax and release the hold on pending tasks. To calm yourself, consider taking a bath, going for a short walk with your dog, or enjoying a tea break by the window. Whether you're sitting before a smiling Buddha statue, beneath a crucifix, using white noise or gentle nature sounds to ward off distractions, or lighting candles to create a tranquil atmosphere, regard your personal time as a *sacred container* for self-care. This space should be seen as an opportunity to become more receptive to behavioral shifts, emotional recalibrations, and fresh perspectives.

Consider having a study partner read the exercises to you or recording them on your phone or another device. This hands-free approach allows you to access unconscious thoughts and emotions more easily. You can also access these exercises at *raydoktor.com/tools* where Dr. Ray will guide you personally.

Fantastic Feedback Exercise

Starting with the Fantastic Feedback exercise is key because mastering feedback is crucial for healthy relationships. Many of us struggle with it due to past negative experiences, such as family arguments that never resolved or emotional expression met with silence. These past events can make us defensive, even with understanding partners who mean us no harm.

1. The Courage to Begin: A Step Into the Unknown

Improving our receptiveness to feedback can enhance our relationships and personal growth. If you become defensive or engage in negative self-judgment, it's important to change these reactions. Viewing the book's content through a negative lens—such as blaming your upbringing or culture, or having self-deprecating thoughts like, "I was stupid, I should have known better" or "Why didn't I say no?"—creates a harmful loop that blocks progress.

Feedback here is not about blame but a neutral tool for improvement. Our goal is to use it constructively for our own well-being, as well as that of our families and communities.

Ask yourself these questions:

What is your relationship to feedback?

_____

How do you interpret feedback?

_____

What does feedback mean to you?

_____

What have you learned about feedback?

_____

How would you prefer to receive feedback?

Allow yourself to answer these questions openly and honestly. Write down your answers in a journal, on your computer, or on your phone.

Your honest responses may unveil common feelings people often experience when receiving feedback. You might feel as if you've done something wrong, or as though you're being judged. Perhaps you worry that you'll appear less attractive to the person providing the feedback, or that you should have already been aware of the issues raised. Becoming aware of a personality trait or communication style that has potentially alienated many people can lead to feelings of regret or a tendency to dwell on the past.

Now, let's proceed to the second part of this exercise—fostering a healthy relationship with feedback. Feedback is a powerful tool; it helps us refine our actions, understand others' feelings, support our children's needs, improve our job performance, and even enhance our intimate relationships. View it as a gift to be gratefully received.

Relax your body, open your heart, and silently recite the following affirmations three times:

Feedback reflects care and recognition of my potential from others.

I welcome feedback as a mirror for personal growth.

Feedback is vital for my self-improvement, happiness, and success.

I embrace feedback to enhance my life and relationships.

Feedback is a tool to refine my behavior and move past old, counterproductive habits.

Feedback reveals what no longer aligns with my personal evolution.

Embracing feedback sustains the passion in my relationships and life.

Feedback is the universe's support on my spiritual journey.
I am cared for.

1. The Courage to Begin: A Step Into the Unknown

Tree of Awareness Grounding Exercise

The grounding exercise that I guided Mary through can also help relax your nervous system. It is especially useful before significant meetings or conversations, or when you feel scattered and want to be more present. Additionally, it serves as an excellent preliminary grounding exercise before you begin any of the exercises provided in this book.

As all life on earth shares a similar biochemistry, standing against a tree with a positive vibration, or even visualizing one, can have beneficial physical effects. Consider a tree's resonance, much like a tuning fork's, assisting our bodies to vibrate at our natural frequency, thereby calming our nervous system.

Lean against a tree that draws you in, or gaze at a tall one outside your window. Alternatively, find an image of a tree in a magazine, or on your computer or phone. I frequently visit a few special trees in my neighborhood. Find your own special tree.

Visualize the tree's roots anchored deep in the earth and its branches reaching for the sky. Regardless of whether you're leaning against a tree or looking at a picture, sense its grounding energy. Let your body harmonize with its calming frequency, drawing nourishment from the earth and light from the sun and sky.

1. The Courage to Begin: A Step Into the Unknown

You are tapping into the ancient wisdom of the tree, a testament to the resilience that survives storms, fires, and changing seasons, still standing tall and flourishing. You recognize that, like this tree, you too have journeyed through life's challenges. These experiences have shaped your heart, nurturing empathy within you and bestowing upon you the wisdom to be of service to those who surround you.

Imagine your thoughts as leaves. Some thoughts, like leaves, are vibrant and large, while others are smaller and faded. Yet, each one is fleeting, just a moment in your ever-expanding consciousness and growth, much like a flourishing tree.

Each thought, a leaf, dances in the gentle breeze, appearing and disappearing without judgment. Those leaves, like certain thoughts that have served their purpose, naturally fall to the ground to be recycled back into the earth, making space for new growth.

With reverence, feel your deep, smooth breath as the life force that fuels the sturdy trunk of the tree, anchoring you firmly in the present moment. As you tune into the rhythm of your breathing, the rise and fall of your chest, you root your awareness into this beautiful, safe moment. It serves as a gentle reminder that you're supported by life itself and love.

Visualize your feet as the roots of the tree, reaching deep into the fertile earth. Let this experience connect you to the life force moving through every cell of your body, tapping into your true vitality.

Feel the tree's mighty energy and its solid, grounding presence flow into you, transforming you into a calm, confident, and grounded being. Inhale and smell the invigorating freshness of nature, letting it rejuvenate you. With each deep, loving breath, you crystallize this grounded state into your consciousness. Hear yourself and your spiritual guides affirming, "You are here. You are amazing. And I love you." As you take another deep, loving breath, you exhale slowly.

When you feel ready, gently return to the present, guiding your focus through eleven intentional, deep breaths. As you open your eyes, imagine experiencing the beauty of the sun for the first time, its warmth softly touching your face, kissing it with healing light. Allow this state of mind, presence, and energy to accompany you throughout the day. Become a living embodiment of love, serenity, clarity, presence, and confidence.

Place both hands over your heart, directing warmth, kindness, and compassion inward. Read the Prayer of Love, Peace, and Light. Speak it aloud and once in silence, allowing its healing words to resonate within you.

Prayer of Love, Peace, and Light

> Love before me, Love behind me, Love at my left, Love at my right, Love above me, Love below me, Love in me, Love in my surroundings, Love to all, Love to the Universe.

> Peace before me, Peace behind me, Peace at my left, Peace at my right, Peace above me, Peace below me, Peace in me, Peace in my surroundings, Peace to all, Peace to the Universe.

> Light before me, Light behind me, Light at my left, Light at my right, Light above me, Light below me, Light in me, Light in my surroundings, Light to all, Light to the Universe.

2
Beyond Invisible Walls: Escaping the Psychological Prison

You exist in a meaningless world until you assign your own meaning to people, places, things, and circumstances. Your emotions, thoughts, beliefs, and experiences are shaped by your unique interpretations. Whether images flicker in your mind, stories unravel, or sensations pulse within you, your experiences are uniquely yours. No one else will perceive or respond exactly as you do, because no one has the same consciousness.

Think of your unique consciousness as the translator that forms perceptions, imparting meaning and feelings to your mind concerning every life experience. Whether it's what you see on social media, the stories shared by friends, or messages from your beloved, everything is filtered through your distinctive consciousness. This process creates impressions and feelings, attributing significance to these collective experiences. Occasionally, these beliefs may be inaccurate, subjective, rooted in fear, or even evolve into distorted perceptions or hidden beliefs.

To understand how perceptions are influenced and shaped by conditions and environments, consider the following scenarios.

A young elephant, tied with a weak rope, struggles to break free but is held back by its small size. As it matures and gains strength, it could easily snap the rope. Yet, past experiences keep it bound, making it

2. Beyond Invisible Walls: Escaping the Psychological Prison

believe it's trapped. This showcases how early encounters and beliefs mold our views, often limiting us even when situations evolve.

Consider flies in a jar. They repeatedly try to escape, hitting the lid. Once the lid is removed, they hesitate to fly out, having been conditioned to feel trapped. This indicates that prolonged constraints can hinder us from seeing new opportunities, even when they're readily available.

Similarly, fish in a tank separated by a partition learn they can't cross to the other side. Even after the barrier is removed, they hesitate, conditioned by the past obstacle. Much like these fish, we can be influenced by prior restrictions.

In the 1999 Invisible Gorilla Experiment by psychologists Daniel Simons and Christopher Chabris, participants tasked with counting basketball passes overlooked a person in a gorilla suit walking through the scene. This highlights how our attention can be narrowly focused, leading to missed details when concentrating on a specific task.

The 1971 Stanford Prison Experiment, led by Dr. Philip Zimbardo, saw college students play the roles of prisoners or guards. Swiftly, guards exhibited authoritarian tendencies, and prisoners displayed distress. This experiment showcased how easily we adapt to given roles, suggesting we can be influenced by our environment and societal expectations, even becoming swayed by collective narratives and social media.

Unconscious Echoes:
The Art of Jennifer's Self-Sabotage

To further illustrate how life experiences can shape negative beliefs, behavioral patterns, and our perceptions through consciousness, here's a case study about Jennifer, a woman who developed *hidden beliefs* to survive her tumultuous childhood:

Jennifer was in a long-distance relationship with Francesco from Italy. To keep their bond strong, they had daily phone calls at a set time, considering their work schedules and regular waking hours. She was talented at painting, so she painted a portrait of Francesco and sent it to him while he slept, eagerly anticipating his response upon waking. When he didn't reply as she had expected, she became anxious. She began to obsess over why Francesco hadn't called back, tormented by thoughts that he might not have liked the painting or that it wasn't good enough, which fueled her self-doubt and insecurities.

Twelve hours later, Francesco finally called. He was unaware of the anxiety Jennifer had been feeling. When she asked him why he hadn't returned her calls, he explained that her painting had deeply touched him. Inspired, he spent the day recording a song for her in the studio. He mentioned he had emailed the audio file to her just before calling her back.

Jennifer was flooded with a mix of anger, gratitude, and embarrassment. Tears streamed down her face as she processed the situation over the phone. While Francesco had poured his heart and soul into the song to express his love and appreciation for Jennifer, his lack of timely communication inadvertently triggered her unresolved insecurities and feelings of being gaslighted.

2. Beyond Invisible Walls: Escaping the Psychological Prison

We might assume that a simple text from Francesco, expressing his enthusiasm about the painting or letting Jennifer know he was fine and would get back to her, could have prevented the entire misunderstanding. However, understanding Jennifer's childhood background makes it easy to recognize that her insecurities might have surfaced regardless. These insecurities could potentially resurface during another instance of miscommunication or a different trigger, even if Francesco had responded more quickly. Here's a glimpse into Jennifer's story:

Through prior psychotherapy, Jennifer had come to know her childhood well. In our coaching sessions, she revealed that her parents had divorced when she was eight. Following the divorce, her father seldom saw her and was emotionally distant. He rarely communicated with her, and neither of her parents were open about the emotional pain they carried from their divorce. Jennifer often saw her mother in distress, retreating to her bedroom while Jennifer played by herself. On knocking to check on her mother, she would invariably receive the same response: "I'm fine."

Whenever Jennifer's father would see her in person, he was never present and was always on his phone. However, he would show interest when Jennifer shared her accomplishments. Her mother eventually began dating several men but was often heartbroken because the relationships were fleeting and challenging. Jennifer said she felt as if she became the parent in the relationship because her mother was emotionally immature.

Understanding Jennifer's childhood and her parents' influence sheds light on her interactions and triggers with Francesco. She was deeply affected by her parents' divorce, notably their lack of transparency, poor coping skills, and emotional distance. Despite years of therapy and open discussions about her challenging childhood with close friends, Jennifer predominantly attracted emotionally unavailable men who were poor communicators.

2. Beyond Invisible Walls: Escaping the Psychological Prison

Jennifer viewed her mother as weak and vowed never to be like her—feeling sorry for herself or relying on men. So, she became an independent and strong businesswoman. She excelled in business but struggled with emotional stability in intimate relationships. To maintain emotional control, she typically opted for casual connections or long-distance relationships unconsciously.

Despite doing all the right things—going to the gym, meditating, attending self-development workshops, and practicing yoga regularly—Jennifer still felt anxious and insecure in relationships. She was consistently triggered by poor communication, whether it was unanswered text messages, partners not expressing their emotions, or awkward silences in conversations.

Let's explore the hidden beliefs that were holding Jennifer back, and how she took personal responsibility to change her emotions, perspectives on herself and relationships, and finally broke through negative behavioral and relationship patterns forever.

Jennifer's Hidden Beliefs

Hidden Belief One:

"Long distance, softer, or younger men are safer." Jennifer unconsciously sought casual relationships with younger, less established men to feel more in control.

Healing:

Jennifer realized that emotional safety stems from taking full responsibility for her feelings. She transitioned from controlling others to trusting herself, alleviating her anxiety.

Hidden Belief Two:

"Vulnerability signifies weakness." Jennifer's guarded demeanor resulted in imbalanced relationships where she constantly gave and rarely received.

2. Beyond Invisible Walls: Escaping the Psychological Prison

Healing:

By releasing her immature emotional ties and expectations of her parents, Jennifer evolved into a healthier adult. This transformation enhanced her trust in herself and others, allowing her to partake in relationships characterized by both giving and receiving.

Hidden Belief Three:

"If I please others, they'll be happy and will want to maintain a relationship with me." By accommodating others, Jennifer believed she could make them content and retain them in her life, mirroring the hope she held for her parents.

Healing:

Jennifer discerned that as long as she learns from each relationship, its longevity doesn't determine its value; it fulfills her soul's mission. She also acknowledged that she cannot be the sole source of someone's happiness—true contentment originates from within.

Hidden Belief Four:

"Men and relationships inherently involve work and sacrifice." Jennifer perceived poor communication as a standard in intimate relationships and frequently dismissed or underestimated warning signs when exploring new romantic prospects.

Healing:

Jennifer came to understand that she had been magnetizing ill-fated relationships because she hadn't delineated her relationship desires. Prior to our coaching, she lacked a lucid perspective on what constitutes a healthy relationship.

Hidden Belief Five:

"I am fundamentally flawed and beyond repair." Even after consulting multiple therapists and partaking in personal growth initiatives, Jennifer felt trapped. She harbored the belief that she was beyond assistance.

Healing:

By energetically and emotionally relinquishing the notion "I am broken," Jennifer dismantled her *invisible wall*, undergoing a transformation where she felt both integrated and fulfilled.

Jennifer's Spectacular New Healthy Relationship

After coaching, Jennifer underwent a significant transformation. She blossomed, radiating positivity and hope. Through the process of reprogramming and rediscovering herself, she became eager to foster a deeper relationship with herself.

Jennifer chose to conclude her long-distance relationship with Francesco. While they parted, she felt no regrets, realizing the relationship had sharpened her understanding of what she wanted in a partner. She yearned for a relationship built on transparency and genuine communication, with a partner who valued her vulnerability and was present. For the first time, she relished her single status, fully embodying her newfound attributes during mindful dating experiences that prioritized honesty and authenticity, both with herself and others.

Approximately fifteen months after embracing her singlehood and venturing out on her own, Jennifer entered a loving, committed relationship with Adam. He too had undergone therapy and delved into self-development following his divorce. Jennifer and Adam's interactions were sincere and deep, with both placing a high value on transparent communication. Their love blossomed, forging a bond that emphasized healing and mutual growth. The couple eventually decided to share a home and marked their love with an intimate ceremony. With their combined focus on growth and dedication, they've now cherished twelve harmonious years of marriage.

2. Beyond Invisible Walls: Escaping the Psychological Prison

Illuminating Our Shadows, Hidden Beliefs, and Silent Traumas

We all have hidden beliefs influenced by our upbringing, culture, traumas, and other life experiences. These hidden beliefs, both positive and negative, help us navigate life's emotional intricacies and safeguard our well-being. They can lurk in the shadows, driving our reactions until we reconcile our past and transform these limiting beliefs.

Swiss psychiatrist Carl Jung emphasized the importance of acknowledging and incorporating these shadows for personal growth, stating, "Everyone carries a shadow, and the less it is embodied in the individual's conscious life, the blacker and denser it is."

Even after years of therapy or self-development programs, some individuals might not experience positive changes. Typically, we address only the tip of the iceberg—symptoms such as avoidance, anxiety, self-doubt, bragging, or over-talking due to nervousness—while neglecting what lies hidden beneath. Additionally, we often focus on unmet expectations and what's not working, blaming our parents or past childhood experiences as excuses for our insecure, reactive behavior.

Repeatedly retelling these stories inevitably activates our nervous system, releases stress in our bodies, and hardwires our neuronal connections to experiences of feeling victimized or out of control, leaving us feeling stuck or as if we've relived the trauma all over again. Merely discussing what we *think* or *feel* is the problem doesn't necessarily lead to genuine transformation and healing. In fact, it often reinforces our negative patterns and disappointing relationship outcomes.

It's also important to remember that we aren't the same individuals we once were, especially after past traumatic events or during childhood. The narratives we create about these experiences might not

2. Beyond Invisible Walls: Escaping the Psychological Prison

be accurate, as our memories fade and our perspectives change over time. Our evolving consciousness reshapes our autobiographical tales, offering new interpretations of our former selves and the experiences we encountered. Our stories are often influenced by others' accounts, photos, or videos. Especially in younger childhood, when we're often in the *theta* brain wave, similar to a dream state, our narratives can merge with television shows, movies, books, and stories shared by others.

For instance, late one night, my son's mother was held at gunpoint outside her apartment complex near her car. Despite her fear, she stayed calm, holding our son, Max, who was three at the time, and handed over her purse to the two young men. At that moment, Max didn't sense any danger; he seemed completely unaware of the gravity of the situation, showing no signs of distress or fear.

Six months later, Max casually mentioned the incident to me, saying that men in "gorilla suits" had taken his mom's purse, as though he was stating a simple fact. However, as he heard more details about the event from others over time, his narrative became increasingly dramatic, seemingly echoing the adults' retellings, such as being told how lucky he was that nothing bad happened to him.

By the time Max was six, after watching a film in which an animated character had his food stolen, he related the past robbery to a friend as if he was fully aware of the whole event. I pointed out to Max that his retelling had evolved, becoming more embellished than his initial, innocent interpretation where he imagined the perpetrators as "gorillas." We all shared a laugh over his dramatic rendition, and he hasn't brought it up in that manner since. What might have been traumatic for many was, for Max, a neutral experience. His interpretation remained untouched by negativity, preserving the innocence of his initial inner dialogue.

I understand that this story may be difficult to accept, particularly if

2. Beyond Invisible Walls: Escaping the Psychological Prison

you're a parent. Your lower-path brain or mama bear instincts might trigger urgent signals like *danger* or *potential death*, urging you to flee or perceive the situation as extremely bad. You might suspect that I influenced my son's perception of the armed robbery. Yet, it's crucial to recognize that what we regard as *memory* is a collaborative construct, influenced by our current state of consciousness, our environment, and the narratives shared by those around us.

The trajectory of our lives, whether we advance or remain in victimization, is influenced by how we interpret and integrate potentially negative experiences and the narratives we cultivate in both our conscious and unconscious minds. The way our perspectives are shaped by our understanding or positive reframing can either propel us forward or keep us anchored to the past.

Many of us develop hidden beliefs following challenges such as witnessing our parents argue frequently, experiencing a house burglary, feeling betrayed by a friend, being sexually violated by a trusted family member, or losing a parent during our toddler years. These experiences can manifest into hidden beliefs such as:

"It's better to stay single than marry."

"Always lock doors; people are untrustworthy."

"Men and women can't be just friends without sexual attraction."

"Growing old means ending up alone."

"All men are predictable."

"Life takes hard work. Nothing comes easy."

2. Beyond Invisible Walls: Escaping the Psychological Prison

"Avoiding sharing how I feel is better than confrontation."

"Trust must be earned to avoid betrayal."

"Money can change one's values."

"For the sake of children, parents should remain together, even if they're constantly fighting."

The presuppositions and hidden beliefs we've unconsciously created in our psyche act as a double-edged sword. While initially serving as survival mechanisms that shield us from emotional distress and help us maintain control, they can also inhibit our personal growth. Take Jennifer, for example. Although she has flourished as an educated, independent, and well-respected individual, her longstanding hidden beliefs—ones that pushed her to surpass her mother's achievements and maintain financial and emotional independence—eventually became barriers to her further evolution.

Jennifer realized that her perception of vulnerability as a weakness and her insistence on being an emotionally independent woman were causing anxiety in her intimate relationships. Her path towards personal growth involved forgiving her parents, reassessing her judgments about her mother, and acknowledging her past feelings of helplessness. In doing so, she redefined emotional vulnerability as a strength.

As a result, Jennifer deepened her connections with Adam, her colleagues, and her friends, understanding that her views on vulnerability and independence were the root cause of her relationship anxieties. By forgiving her parents and reevaluating her judgments, she embraced vulnerability as a strength.

2. Beyond Invisible Walls: Escaping the Psychological Prison

The key to transforming hidden beliefs is to embrace both our shadows and our light, dispelling polarization. This involves nurturing connections instead of isolating parts of ourselves we don't like, whether they stem from difficult childhood experiences, traumas, or personality traits we find unappealing.

Typical Sequence of Healing Evolution

If you're at the onset of your healing journey or, like Jennifer, find yourself stagnant despite seeking guidance from therapists or coaches, attending retreats, or drawing upon self-development exercises, the issue often lies in unidentified and non-neutralized hidden beliefs.

These unresolved beliefs can continue to create emotional disturbances. Moreover, if you haven't fully integrated a fresh mindset or pursued action aligned with your desired change—be it speaking your truth, dedicating time at the gym, writing that book, setting clear boundaries, or adopting a healthier diet—you aren't truly embodying the transformations you aspire to.

On our journey of emotional and psychological healing, many of us follow a similar pattern. To gain a deeper understanding of the healing process and the structure of consciousness, consider why we might feel better at times yet still feel stuck at other times. Explore how to break free from this cycle by examining the following sequence:

1. Acceptance:

You are no longer in denial. Perhaps after a breakup, you recognize a recurring theme—multiple partners highlighting your anger issues. When you relocate to a new city yet find the same problems and personalities, you begin to discern that the issue might be with you, not them. Now, there's an acknowledgment of the problem and a desire to address it.

2. Initiating Conversations about the Problem:

You start discussing your problems, be it casually at the gym, with your hairdresser, or among friends. There's a thirst for understanding. You delve into research, perhaps watching YouTube videos to find relatable stories, purchasing books on the subject, or listening to self-help podcasts recommended by peers.

3. Seek Support:

When there's a lingering feeling of being stuck, you desire further guidance. Recognizing the possible biases of people close to you or noticing that many in your circle struggle with similar challenges, you consider professional aid. This might take the form of a coach, therapist, or participation in healing retreats and workshops.

4. Retell Past Stories:

Perhaps a memory resurfaces of your father leaving or an inappropriate encounter with a babysitter. These recollections help you make connections, like your challenges with intimacy, or maybe you learned to yell from one of your parents instead of communicating calmly. You recall the first time you felt shy in front of your kindergarten class and connect this event to your current fear of public speaking.

NOTE: Retelling past stories is typically part of the healing sequence where individuals, like Jennifer, struggle to move forward in their growth. They may understand how past events have affected them but fail to move beyond this realization to actual learning and improvement. Real change involves uncovering hidden beliefs—those deep-seated mental scripts—and then actively rewriting them.

5. Transforming Hidden Beliefs:

This involves reframing past experiences and aligning with a more desired state of consciousness and emotions. For instance, the belief "I was abandoned by my parents" can expand to "My parents couldn't love me because they couldn't love themselves, so I'm going to love myself anyway and also accept others' love, even if I didn't have the

2. Beyond Invisible Walls: Escaping the Psychological Prison

best childhood." Similarly, statements like "I was awkward due to bullying" can transform into the compassionate "Hurt people hurt people," which leads to the expansion, "I consistently encounter kindness because I allow others to be authentically themselves."

Instead of saying "It's better to stay single than to marry" to avoid conflict or toxic relationships like our parents', we could clarify the real issue with "I was always afraid my relationships would end up like my parents'." By taking personal responsibility, we can become more authentic and lean into relationships that support the new version of ourselves. We can affirm, "I create the relationships I prefer and maintain healthy boundaries."

If we've struggled with jealousy, seen infidelity in our parents, or experienced it ourselves, we might form the belief, "All men are cheaters." However, this isn't a universal truth but a reflection of our experiences, or those of our parents or partners, who had poor boundaries. By taking responsibility, we could admit, "I overlooked the red flags because I was lonely or needy." This awareness can grow into, "When I'm true to myself, I make good decisions and feel confident."

Maybe one of our parents was often absent or inconsistent, which left us feeling disappointed and reluctant to trust others. This might lead us to adopt the belief, "Trust must be earned." While we may think we're protecting our hearts, as healed adults, we can begin to lower our guard. In doing so, we open ourselves to people who are trustworthy and committed to a healthy relationship. Instead of clinging to the belief "Trust must be earned," which keeps people at a distance, we can embrace a new perspective: "There are good people in the world, just like me, who I would love to spend my time with."

There's a chance you're skeptical that overcoming something that has defined your entire life could be too easy, as if we're just sweeping a bad experience under the rug. You might feel that because you've

2. Beyond Invisible Walls: Escaping the Psychological Prison

struggled for so long with an issue, healing will require a tremendous effort and time, and these beliefs can seem true if you believe them. In other words, if your imagination has kept you bound to a traumatic experience or years of neglect from childhood, it also has the power to create new, positive life and relationship maps within your consciousness. This can result in your biology emitting happy neurochemicals, your relationships reflecting positive changes through transparent communication, and your demeanor showing how trusting, confident, and open you are to friends, family, and strangers.

It takes no effort or personal responsibility to cling to beliefs like "They should have known better." But if they truly knew better, the negative event wouldn't have happened. Blaming others, dwelling on past wrongs, or things we can't change today is like trying to start a car we know has no gas. Imagine getting angry every day because the car won't start, yet each morning, we choose to get back into the car, expecting to reach our destination. When it doesn't start, we get frustrated, blaming the car, gas prices, or insurance, instead of taking the bus, riding a bike, or simply walking to get gas.

Your negative thinking about yourself, life, and relationships is like that car with no gas. If you hang onto negative beliefs and self-doubt, your life and relationships won't improve. It's like trying to travel without fuel. You must change your thoughts and beliefs for a different and better outcome. Taking responsibility might be tough at first, but it frees you from letting your past control your present and future. Sure, life isn't about the destination, but the journey should be fun, adventurous, filled with new experiences, and create good memories you'll never want to forget.

Uncovering Hidden Belief Exercise

Let's dig into a hidden belief you might have. To keep it simple, focus on just one issue. Although I've emphasized not blaming others and

2. Beyond Invisible Walls: Escaping the Psychological Prison

taking personal responsibility for our feelings, it's crucial to be authentic when uncovering hidden beliefs—even if that means sounding angry or judgmental. This authenticity helps you connect with your true self. Writing down your thoughts and feelings often leads to greater clarity. For example, if you realize you're angry, you'll likely find that you want to feel happy instead. If you feel controlled, you probably yearn for freedom. And if you're blaming someone or something from the past, it's a sign you may want to let that go and move forward.

Step One:

Identify your problem in its most raw and authentic form. Use the first words that come to mind, like:

"Tony is such a jerk!"

_____

"They're judging me without even knowing me."

_____

"My parents never really loved me."

_____

"I always mess up; I'm a failure."

_____

"How could she disrespect me like that?"

Your turn now. Keep it simple. Share the first thought that comes to mind about what's bothering you, what issue from the past lingers, or how you currently feel about someone. Limit it to two sentences.

Step Two:

Own the feelings, thoughts, and judgments you form when you hold these beliefs. Notice how your body responds, how your breathing changes, the behaviors you exhibit, the assumptions you make, and any other physical sensations that come up when you engage with these thoughts or situations such as:

2. Beyond Invisible Walls: Escaping the Psychological Prison

"Tony is such a jerk!": Anger and irritation are the immediate emotions. If harbored long-term, these feelings may turn into resentment, causing tension and emotional drain.

"They're judging me without even knowing me.": This belief can create a sense of insecurity and defensiveness, and possibly lead to social anxiety or withdrawal from social situations to avoid judgment.

"My parents never really loved me.": Deep-rooted sadness and a sense of abandonment could plague the individual. This might lead to chronic low self-esteem and difficulties forming healthy relationships.

"I always mess up; I'm a failure.": A feeling of inadequacy dominates, leading to despair. If internalized, this belief could result in depression and even contribute to a self-sabotaging behavior pattern.

"How could she disrespect me like that?": Initial feelings of betrayal and indignation may lead to increased guardedness in relationships, possibly resulting in trust issues and relational conflicts.

Step Three:

Let's dig into any hidden beliefs that might be holding you back. These beliefs could create recurring patterns or feelings that make you feel stuck. Whether the issue is current, momentary, or rooted in the past, identifying these hidden beliefs is the first step to revealing the unconscious scripts in our minds. Once we're aware, we can start making changes. Here are some examples:

"Tony is such a jerk!" *Hidden Belief*: "People who are difficult make my life worse, and I have no control over it."

2. Beyond Invisible Walls: Escaping the Psychological Prison

"They're judging me without even knowing me." *Hidden Belief*: "I am misunderstood, and people are unfair to me, which justifies my defensiveness."

"My parents never really loved me." *Hidden Belief*: "I am unlovable and that's why even those who should care for me don't."

"I always mess up; I'm a failure." *Hidden Belief*: "I am inherently flawed and can't do things right, which means I'll never succeed."

"How could she disrespect me like that?" *Hidden Belief*: "My value is tied to how others treat me, and her actions have diminished my worth."

Step Four:

Now let's shift focus to what you'd like to experience in your life, relationships, and communication. We'll craft new positive beliefs to counteract the negative ones. This is your chance to flip the script, reframe your thoughts, and take responsibility for how you want to feel and live. If negative beliefs can affect you, so can positive ones. Here, you're taking control of how the situation impacted you, including your unhealed areas and the coping mechanisms you've used to survive. You're now forming new beliefs and guiding principles that align with your current state of consciousness. Here are some examples:

"People who are difficult make my life worse, and I have no control over it."
New Belief: "I can control how I respond and maintain my inner peace."

"I am misunderstood, and people are unfair to me, which justifies my defensiveness."
New Belief: "My worth is determined by me."

"I am unlovable and that's why even those who should care for me don't."
New Belief: "I am worthy of love and care."

"I am inherently flawed and can't do things right, which means I'll never succeed."
New Belief: "I embrace growth and learning, understanding that each step, even missteps, bring me closer to success."

"My value is tied to how others treat me, and her actions have diminished my worth."
New Belief: "My self-worth is intrinsic and determined by how I perceive myself."

Once you've crafted your new positive life statement, make it a habit to read it aloud or silently to yourself daily. The beginning of the day is best, but also consider doing it before you go to sleep. Consider performing the Tree of Awareness Grounding Exercise from chapter one to help put you in the right mindset to recite your new life statement or engage in other activities where you feel more relaxed, open, and receptive.

Continue to read your new positive life statement until you notice a shift in your behavior and emotions. You might even forget what originally bothered you, indicating a change in your consciousness. Sometimes, you'll experience immediate relief just by going through this process once. Whether you call these new statements affirmations or life scripts, they're not just words. They are simple yet powerful

2. Beyond Invisible Walls: Escaping the Psychological Prison

sentences that connect you to your true feelings, bodily sensations, and mindset. This integrated approach shapes your physical reality through your newfound spiritual self-awareness.

3
Mental Blueprint: Decoding the Structures of Belief

One of the best ways to understand the origins of our beliefs, attitudes, personality, and coping mechanisms is to examine key influences during our formative years. This helps us make sense of how we communicate, solve problems, and show up in various contexts like relationships, business, health, and spirituality. It also sheds light on our cultural and collective beliefs.

To deepen your understanding of your relationships and self, I've designed a simple exercise focused on eleven key life influencers common across cultures. This exercise helps you explore how your consciousness, fears, and beliefs were formed.

After each influencer, I provide reflective questions. Feelings may surface as you engage with the exercise. Pause, breathe deeply, and place your hands on your heart to reflect on each question. Approach this process with curiosity and openness, free from judgment. The aim is to examine the experiences that may have shaped your beliefs. Compassionate observation can help diffuse any emotional charge tied to these experiences.

3. Mental Blueprint: Decoding the Structures of Belief

The Eleven Collective Life Influencers

The Prenatal Period:

Our first emotional experiences in this life begin in our mother's womb. Everything she feels, we feel. Without conscious discrimination, we may not know what her feelings are and what ours are as we experience our mother through the placenta, nervous system, and energy body.

Her experiences become our experiences, including if she's upset with our father or her parents, feels pressure about college, or is trying to figure out how to pay the bills. Basically, if she feels fear, we feel fear. If she lacks trust in herself and feels unsafe in her environment, we will be influenced by her interpretation of her experiences. Her emotions can feel like thunderclouds, as if her womb is our universe. If she breathes in calmness, places her hands over her belly, and sings to us with unconditional love, this can provide the safety and trust needed for a supportive entry into the world when we take our first breaths.

We are a collaboration of our mother's pregnancy. Everything that happens during this time is relevant and pertinent to the life themes we've chosen to explore. We are both teachers and students to each other in this co-creation.

3. Mental Blueprint: Decoding the Structures of Belief

Reflect on the following questions to bring more awareness to your prenatal period:

What do you remember about your birth?

What were you told about your mother's pregnancy?

What was your mother experiencing during her pregnancy?

What were your mother's relationships like during her pregnancy?

How do you think your mother felt about herself during her pregnancy?

Caregivers:

We unconsciously model many of our behaviors, beliefs, conflict-resolution styles, communication patterns, survival mechanisms, and life philosophies by spending time with our parents, grandparents, uncles, or whoever we spend a lot of time with. We learn by observing and interacting with them. It's as if we're sponges, absorbing their emotions, facial gestures, humor, sarcasm, cynicism, optimism, pessimism, their communication in relationships, how they cope with stress, what brings them joy and happiness, how they see the world and their purpose, and how they share their story with us.

We're not blaming or vilifying our caregivers but are objectively acknowledging our experiences, what we were often exposed to, and how life felt to us. For example, if our mother was a germaphobe and constantly cleaning, we might be sticklers for hygiene and maintain a tidy home. If our father drove his car aggressively like a New York cab driver, honking his horn and yelling at other drivers, we might also find ourselves impatient behind the wheel. If our mother was

3. Mental Blueprint: Decoding the Structures of Belief

often angry and reactive, our spouse might tell us that we're hotheads as well. If our father was unhappy with his job and only worked to support the family, even if he was loving towards us, he could have been experiencing depression, making our home feel unhappy. This could have influenced our feelings about life, work, and relationships. If there was a lack of transparency in our home growing up, or if we didn't feel safe, we could have developed trust issues.

As we expand our consciousness and recognize the life themes we came to explore before our conception, we will remember who we really are and how we chose to participate in our own lives.

Reflect on the following questions to better understand the influences of your caregivers:

What style of communication did you witness in your home?

What was the temperament and mood (stressful, loving, or uncommunication) of your home?

As a child, how did you feel most of the time?

What was important to your parents, and what did they talk about often?

How did your parents feel about themselves?

Social Media:

Whatever is making headlines, be it a war, an event like the Academy Awards, a school shooting, high gas prices, a controversial music video, or a political scandal, it's guaranteed to be talked about and generate engagement and views on social media platforms.

3. Mental Blueprint: Decoding the Structures of Belief

We face numerous social, health, economic, and environmental problems, and our experiences and perceptions of reality can be influenced by what our friends, family, and community members pay attention to and discuss. Our understanding of the world is shaped by the media we consume, such as the news, sitcoms, Facebook, Instagram, YouTube, and TikTok, as well as the subcultures and social norms within our communities.

As children, our beliefs and values are heavily influenced by our family and the environments we grow up in. We adopt our parents' political views, religious beliefs, and attitudes towards topics like gun control and abortion. However, it's important to remember that these views may not be universal and can vary greatly from one community to another, even from one country to another.

By being aware of the power of social media to shape our perspectives, we can start to make more conscious and deliberate choices about what we pay attention to and what feels true and important to us.

Reflect on the following questions to recognize how social media could have made life impressions:

Do you remember what you watched on television with your family?

─────────

What major events happened during your childhood and were all over the news?

─────────

Can you recall what was popular, what you liked, and what you shared with your friends?

─────────

What songs did you sing, what were they about, and what did you daydream about?

─────────

3. Mental Blueprint: Decoding the Structures of Belief

> Who were your role models, heroes,
> and celebrities you liked, and why?

Life Experiences:

Because we experienced life a certain way, we might believe this is the way life is for everyone. Our experiences may lead us to form negative beliefs, such as "Trust no one," "Men cheat," "It's not safe to walk alone," or "We need to fend for ourselves." For example, if we've had multiple experiences with cheating partners or been lied to, we might develop a distrustful attitude towards relationships.

Growing up, we may have had to constantly move and make new friends, which can lead us to believe that it's best not to get close to others. As a result, we might find ourselves relocating frequently as adults, even if it makes us feel uncomfortable. If we grew up in a neighborhood with high crime rates, we may become hypervigilant and suspicious, even if we're in a safe environment as adults. This can lead us to advise others to always be careful and lock their doors.

Our imagination is creative, and life experiences often have multiple truths, interpretations, and lessons. There are many ways to understand and process each experience as our consciousness continues to evolve. By directing our awareness and taking personal responsibility to consciously choose the higher road, we integrate learnings from negative experiences, allowing us to grow and steer our lives in a positive direction without being shackled by the past.

Reflect on the following questions to see how life experiences have shaped your beliefs:

> What life experiences have shaped you through fear or love?
>
> ----------
>
> How did you cope with these experiences and
> what safety measures did you take?
>
> ----------

What challenges did you consistently face growing up?

What feelings did you often have during your childhood?

What are the key life lessons and beliefs you adopted from your childhood?

Education:

We're educated by parents, teachers, books, news, science, research, articles, and journals about what happened, why it happened, what it means, what the outcome is, and why things are the way they are. However, it's important to note that the information presented to us may be influenced by the personal beliefs, experiences, and consciousness of the messenger.

Many educational institutions, such as schools, sororities, and fraternities, have underlying beliefs, shadows, and cultural norms that can influence our beliefs. The history, science, and religion taught to us may not be entirely accurate, often influenced and altered by political and religious agendas. As new discoveries are made, fields like science, history, anthropology, and medicine continuously evolve. As new discoveries are made, fields like science, history, anthropology, and medicine are in a constant state of evolution. This continuous expansion of knowledge and technology should be integrated into our education and worldview.

Parents and other educational forums should not only teach children how to think and feel for themselves but also how we're all connected to each other and to nature. A holistic approach to education should also emphasize the impact of self-awareness on our beliefs, behaviors, and actions. By combining self-awareness with education, we can maintain an open mind and continue to grow through new discoveries and expanding consciousness. This approach leads to wisdom and

3. Mental Blueprint: Decoding the Structures of Belief

a deeper understanding of humble life experiences, allowing us to embody what we've learned and share it with others.

Reflect on the following questions to understand your formal and life education:

What did you learn growing up that you never questioned?

Do you remember any biases in your teachers, educators, or parents?

Did you ever learn something that didn't make sense to you, but you still went along with it because you had to graduate?

What was the culture and collective beliefs in your school?

Where do you turn to for new information today and how do you determine its accuracy?

Religion and Spirituality:

Most religions aim to instill values, conduct, and ethics within a culture, yet they often fall short of fully embodying their spiritual teachings and translating them into human living. Historically, many religions were intertwined with governance, serving as instruments for societal control and manipulation. Thus, teachings were often crafted to shape cultural thinking, behavior, and emotions deliberately.

It's important to remember that ancient spiritual teachings were shaped by the collective understanding and limitations of their societies, including misconceptions like the belief that the earth was flat. These teachings, originally shared orally, have been subject to reinterpretation and distortion over time by various interpreters, institutions, and authorities. Teachers' personal histories, experiences, and cultural contexts can also influence these teachings, sometimes

3. Mental Blueprint: Decoding the Structures of Belief

leading to misinterpretations and alterations that conform to societal norms or support discriminatory practices. For example, in a society where women are seen as subordinate to men, spiritual teachings might be twisted to support biased legislation and social control.

When spirituality intertwines with dogma, it can be imposed through force and fear, leading to judgment rooted in self-righteousness. Instead of being empowered by love from entities like Jesus, God, Allah, source energy, or the Great Spirit, fear takes hold, blocking the path to heartfelt compassion.

One doesn't need religion or external approval to reach higher states of consciousness and love. Individuals might connect to spirituality through profound love, like that for a child, or through meditation, prayer, chanting, yoga, gardening, dancing, singing, plant medicine, or transformational workshops. Regardless of how we integrate our spiritual beliefs and healing practices—be it yoga with Christianity or another blend—we can all embrace compassion and unity without judging ourselves or others.

Reflect on the following questions to bring more clarity and understanding of spirituality:

> What was your upbringing in religion and spirituality like?
>
> ---------
>
> What spiritual traditions did your family and culture practice?
>
> ---------
>
> Do you feel comfortable or resistant regarding your spiritual upbringing?
>
> ---------
>
> What are your beliefs about spirituality today?
>
> ---------
>
> Do you have daily rituals that help you connect to love, happiness, and spirit?

3. Mental Blueprint: Decoding the Structures of Belief

Gossip:

As social creatures, we often gravitate towards those who share our opinions and beliefs. When people commiserate with us, we may feel validated and seen. For instance, if our family and friends talk about people, money, politics, religion, life perspectives, and have the same opinions as us, we may believe that everyone thinks like us and that our opinions are truths.

We may judge those who don't share our values and beliefs, but only communicating with people we like can make us narrow-minded. We don't have to agree with or accept a person's opinions or actions, but it's crucial to experience contrast, different opinions and personalities, and even some pain, to aid in our growth and development of new self-awareness.

While commiserating with others about our judgments may make us feel seen and heard, gossiping is a low form of personal responsibility and drains our energy. It rarely creates the outcomes we desire and instead perpetuates feelings of victimization, judgment, and helplessness.

Talking about things or people we dislike can be a starting point to discover what we prefer, but eventually, we need to take personal responsibility. Instead of staying stuck in negative talk, we can take action to move forward. Asking ourselves questions such as, "What do I really want?" "What do I really want to talk about?" or "What healthy actions can I take?" can help us shift from gossip to integrity, compassion, and conscious leadership.

Reflect on the following questions to gain a deeper understanding of the type of conversations you often have:

What do you typically discuss with friends and family?

_____

Are there specific people, situations, or things
you often complain about?

Do you participate more in negative or positive talk?

How would your day be different if you only spoke about things that made you happy?

If you were to take positive action instead of complaining or blaming, what would you do?

Culture:

We are each born into unique families, communities, and cultures that come with their own rules, beliefs, and views which we're taught to accept. As children dependent on others for survival and emotional support, we learn behaviors like sarcasm, smiling, and crying to meet our needs, sometimes hiding our true feelings to gain approval. Our sense of safety and belonging, so vital to our family and community, may require this, often leading us to internalize guilt and fear as a price for feeling included.

Families have shunned and disowned members for not adhering to their rules, and those who don't follow their culture's expectations and beliefs (such as arranged marriages, religion, gender roles, having children, etc.) may face ostracism. Just because our ancestors have believed and practiced something for hundreds of years doesn't make it right or healthy. The lack of acceptance and tolerance can cause harm and carry generational trauma.

Traditions lacking growth potential often face cultural breakdown, especially among the young. Outdated beliefs can't keep up with our evolving consciousness and new aspirations. While many traditions offer valuable lessons, they also have their darker sides. By acknowledging both, we can break free from cultural norms that don't serve our authentic selves. Instead of letting culture dictate

3. Mental Blueprint: Decoding the Structures of Belief

who we are, we can reclaim our spiritual birthright and discover our true selves. This integration enriches our culture, enabling collective thriving.

Reflect on the following questions to examine your culture, traditions, and outdated beliefs:

Do you disagree with any aspects of your culture or traditions?

Have you ever held back being your authentic self to avoid conflict?

Do you feel like you have lived someone else's life rather than your own?

Are there still expectations placed on you by your family?

How would you confidently live your life if your culture didn't agree with you?

Emotional Trauma:

Everyone processes stress, challenges, and change differently. We each cope with experiences like war, car accidents, health issues, sexual abuse, bullying, racism, alcoholism, or persistent childhood neglect in our own ways. Our personal philosophies, skills, and the meanings we assign to these events can either leave us scarred for life or help us define a healthy character in a positive way. It is not the event itself that defines emotional trauma, but rather our interpretation, integration, and the conversations we have afterward that shape our experience.

Most people who are exposed to disturbing experiences can adapt and continue with their normal daily functions without developing mental disorders. However, if the emotional trauma was confusing, ongoing, or occurred within a family member, such as sexual abuse where safety was once felt, healing and moving forward can be more challenging. Not only will we need to heal from the negative experience, but we may also develop trust issues with others and ourselves.

This can further complicate things and lead to a loss of trust in our decisions and healing process. Unconsciously, we may not even trust a therapist or coach. Our sense of self and how this *self* functions in relation to the world may be shattered in response to emotional trauma.

We may avoid future relationships or become hypervigilant by always locking our doors and never walking alone. When it comes to doing new things or going to unfamiliar places, we may worry excessively and develop a constant need for details. If we get stuck in the unconscious patterns of trying to control every situation and person, we may miss out on the unexpected newness of life's surprises and relationships.

Remembering *who we truly are versus what happened to us* starts by acknowledging that we're not confined by our past, emotions, or beliefs. While experiences may have hurt and shaped us, it's not the event or the perpetrator that dictates who we become or how we live. Embracing our hurts without resistance or blame lets us release inner tension. When we integrate the lessons and growth into our new *becoming*, we evolve into something even greater.

Reflect on the following questions to shed light on any unresolved emotions and resentment you might be carrying:

Have there been any emotionally traumatic experiences that have impacted your life?

What beliefs have you created after these negative experiences?

What is your relationship with trusting yourself and others?

3. Mental Blueprint: Decoding the Structures of Belief

How might your life be different if the traumatic experience had not occurred?

How could your life be better if you embraced today and let go of yesterday?

Gender Roles:

In various cultures, masculine and feminine traits are often linked to specific roles, such as men working while women care for the children. We may hold preconceived beliefs about how men or women should behave emotionally and physically. For example, men who are not fond of strong women or who don't believe in equality may make chauvinistic remarks. Conversely, some women may have expectations that men should be strong, masculine, bearded, hard-working, and protective. If a husband fails to meet these expectations, his wife might tell him to "grow some balls and be a real man."

Gender roles, attitudes, and lifestyles are often exploited through social media and used for consumerism. We are told what clothes, makeup, attitudes, lifestyles, and behaviors are more attractive for men or women. Many of us are judged on our physical appearance, tone of voice, and the way we walk and move our bodies, along with the masculine and feminine characteristics associated with gender roles. But what if we don't identify with stereotypical male or female characteristics and are more androgynous?

Whether born male or female, we must ask, "Do anatomy, appearance, sexuality, or society define us, or is it our responsibility to connect with our true essence?" Achieving sexual equality may start with education on embodying a balanced spectrum of masculine and feminine energies. Western societies have been largely shaped by patriarchal views on gender roles, family, and life, characterized by exclusivity, duality, and competition.

Imagine a world where we are valued for our unique essence and fluid mix of masculine and feminine traits. Being labeled as man or woman might carry no emotional weight, serving only to describe our anatomy at birth. By embracing diverse expressions of healthy masculinity and femininity, we'd boost confidence and reduce identity issues.

Reflect on the following questions to understand how you embody your essential masculine and feminine traits:

What expectations were placed on gender roles in your culture?

Did your family have expectations for you as a boy or girl?

Did one of your parents exhibit predominantly more masculine or feminine traits?

How did you feel about your masculinity or femininity growing up?

How comfortable are you now with your masculine and feminine traits?

False Presuppositions:

All of us have been exposed to predetermined beliefs and assumptions about people, relationships, money, health, race, situations, and even parenting. We have unconsciously adopted these presuppositions as truths, rather than discovering if they are true through personal experiences.

We often learn false presuppositions from those with whom we spend more time. Sometimes they are innocent and might have good

3. Mental Blueprint: Decoding the Structures of Belief

intentions, but they are not always true. For example, when I lived in an apartment and wanted a dog, my father said, "A dog needs a yard." It is true that a dog needs to take walks outside, but many dog owners live happily with their dogs in apartments, and I deprived myself of being a dog owner.

Parents trying to protect their daughters, especially a mother who was sexually violated might tell her young daughter, "You know you can't trust boys because they only want one thing." We often hear that relationships take a lot of work and require compromises, but this is not always true. Healthy people who choose healthy partners have better communication and easier relationships.

Generational trauma, especially for immigrants who escaped tyranny, might still not feel safe in a new country. They might tell their children not to stand out and to be vigilant with everyone they meet. Our grandparents might have lived through the Great Depression and worked very hard to cover their bills, and they might still say that life is tough, and you must work hard.

Some intellectual parents want the best for their children and perpetuate the belief that "education comes first." As a result, their children's worthiness becomes about getting into an Ivy League school, rather than pursuing happiness and their own unique expression.

Many of us might share the same experiences and outcomes, but this doesn't make a belief an inherent truth. What if we have created these common experiences, such as difficult relationships, money struggles, and poor health, because we have unconsciously subscribed to these false presuppositions? If we play baseball and are predetermined that we are going to strike out when it's our turn to bat, wouldn't our belief influence the outcome?

The cause of many of our problems is our unexamined false beliefs, not because life is set up for us to fail. Those who loved us may have had good intentions by teaching us about life, but it is important to discover life for ourselves and no longer be passive passengers. We need to take

3. Mental Blueprint: Decoding the Structures of Belief

the driver's seat and steer our own beliefs towards the best feelings, outcomes, and learning.

Reflect on the following questions to explore any false presumptions you might believe and act out:

What do you remember being constantly told to you as a child?

_____

Were there direct comments and life philosophies shared with you that made an impression?

_____

Could you see how those closest to you live their lives by their beliefs without ever questioning them?

_____

Do you find yourself saying the same things your caregivers said to you to others, including your children?

_____

If you could change any of these negative false presuppositions you believe in, what would you tell yourself and others now?

Return to Love Exercise

Some people find it difficult to accept that their caregivers did their best, particularly when neglect or abuse occurred. A more balanced view could be, "They acted based on what they knew, not necessarily what was right." Recognizing that our parents and ancestors were shaped by their own experiences can foster compassion and the understanding that they could only give what they themselves had received.

The key is to take personal responsibility to love and accept ourselves better than we were loved growing up. The struggle with self-acceptance often arises from our ongoing negative self-talk, rather than a lack of past love.

3. Mental Blueprint: Decoding the Structures of Belief

The Return to Love Exercise aims to unearth outdated beliefs and interrupt cycles of generational trauma and unhealthy relationship patterns. It encourages us to reevaluate our historical relationship to love and acceptance and redefine what love means to us now. Simply set a ten-minute timer and quickly complete these ten sentence stems, trusting your initial, unconscious responses.

1. Love means …
2. My family taught me that love meant …
3. I received love when I …
4. I didn't receive love when I …
5. I needed my parents' love when I …
6. I needed to be loved when I …
7. I wished I had been loved when I …
8. Without love, I …
9. When I feel love, I …
10. When I feel love, I can …

Review your answers with curiosity, regardless of what you wrote. Whether love was withheld or not, you'll discover the hidden beliefs you associate with love. Your responses may reveal what you're currently experiencing in relationships, what you feel is missing, and perhaps the conditions you've imposed in relationships to protect yourself from future hurt.

As an example, your responses might include:

1. Love equals pain to me.
2. My family taught me that love has to be earned.
3. I received love when I achieved good grades.
4. I didn't receive love when I disagreed with my parents.
5. I craved my parents' love when I was in college.

3. Mental Blueprint: Decoding the Structures of Belief

6. I sought love when my father remarried.
7. I wished for love when I felt ashamed.
8. I feel lonely without love.
9. Love gives me confidence.
10. Love helps me regulate my emotions better.

Similar to the Uncovering Hidden Belief Exercise in chapter two, we're going to transform your responses into positive present-tense affirmations, such as:

1. "Love means I will get hurt" becomes, "I am safe to receive and give love."
2. "My family taught me that love must be earned" becomes, "I am loved unconditionally."
3. "I received love when I got good grades" becomes, "I receive love every day because I am love."
4. "I didn't receive love when I disagreed with my parents" becomes, "I am authentic and loved for who I am."
5. "I craved my parents' love when I was in college" becomes, "All my life experiences have shaped me into the loving person I am today."
6. "I sought love when my father remarried" becomes, "I am seen for who I truly am."
7. "I wished for love when I felt ashamed" becomes, "Every cell in my body is worthy of love at all times."
8. "I feel lonely without love" becomes, "I appreciate life, love, and sometimes the unexpected, allowing me to continue to grow."
9. "Love makes me feel confident" becomes, "I become more confident every day."
10. "Love helps me manage my emotions better" becomes, "I am emotionally resilient and feel peace in my heart."

3. Mental Blueprint: Decoding the Structures of Belief

Here are some streamlined tips for creating effective positive affirmations and life scripts:

- Identify stressors like work stress and reframe them into positive terms, like "I create peace wherever I am."
- Always use the present tense: Instead of saying "I will have a fulfilling job," say "I have a fulfilling job."
- Frame affirmations positively, avoiding phrases like "I don't want."
- Start with affirmations that resonate with you now and gradually progress. For example, instead of jumping to "I forgive my parents," you might start with "I'm in the process of forgiving."

Repeat these affirmations and life scripts each morning and night, or whenever you need a reminder. Put notes in your car, on your bathroom mirror, or other places where you'll see them. Say them when you're open and receptive and continue until you achieve the change you desire.

Remember, this is a journey. Be patient with yourself as you adapt to these positive shifts. While you can't change others, you can change how you perceive your world, empowering you to be unlimited in your life and relationships.

4
The Illusion of Safety: Revealing Hidden Benefits

Sometimes the barrier to change is a hidden *secondary gain*. For example, staying in a toxic relationship might ensure bills are paid, or sabotaging one's health can lead to collecting disability from a disliked job. Others may resist change to maintain a social image and avoid criticism. Whether it's fear of the unknown, a job that boosts your status but conflicts with your values, or a preference for logic over vulnerability, these secondary gains offer a false sense of control and safety.

What if You Believe That Making Positive Changes in Your Life Could Jeopardize Your Reputation, Livelihood, or Financial Stability?

Beliefs such as "No one else will hire me," "I won't earn as much as I do now," "I'm afraid of losing financial stability," "I have a family to support," "What if I'm not accepted," "I'm too old," or "I'm lucky to have this job" are some of the hidden limiting beliefs that could keep you from embracing growth.

Sometimes, people stay in unfulfilling jobs for the secondary gains of comfort and security they provide, along with the perks of respect and status. Such inauthenticity often leads to inner conflict, manifesting in physical, emotional, and spiritual symptoms like high blood pressure, anxiety, or a sense of emptiness.

While it's natural to worry about financial stability, especially if others depend on you, inaction keeps you misaligned with your true self and unhappy. Failing to make changes like speaking up, furthering your education, or leaving a job that doesn't serve you can negatively impact other areas of your life. By addressing underlying fears around scarcity or unworthiness, you can confidently make positive changes, despite challenges and the potential for disappointing others.

What if There's Neglect, Sexual Abuse, or Someone We Love and Dislike at the Same Time?

If there has been neglect, sexual abuse, or a situation where we love and dislike someone at the same time, it can be challenging to forgive and move forward. Especially when the abuse was sexual and from a family member, it can create a complex mix of emotions, including love, confusion, hurt, connection, and betrayal. This can be even more difficult if the abuse occurred multiple times, both in childhood and as an adult.

Survivors of trauma often live with walls up, feeling hypervigilant about their safety and avoiding close relationships. Even if they appear successful with a good home, relationships, and respect from others, they may still feel unhappy. They may feel numb and not present, even if they have financial success.

Another barrier to healing for those who have been abused or traumatized is the belief that they need to forgive the perpetrator. Some feel that if they heal, the perpetrator escapes justice, creating a sense of unfairness. They may cling to hidden beliefs like, "If he goes unpunished, he'll hurt someone else," "I can't forget what he did," or "I can't comprehend his actions."By maintaining a victim stance, individuals may find a hidden secondary gain: avoiding personal responsibility for the outcomes of their lives. Blaming the perpetrator, or external circumstances, becomes a familiar path and is often perceived as easier than undertaking the difficult work of self-improvement..

Letting go of control often involves releasing our *victim identity*, a label that might have defined us for years. This could elicit hidden beliefs such as, "Who am I without this trauma?" or "Now I actually have to discuss this in therapy, which I don't want to do." If our entire sense of self is built around being a victim and maintaining control for protection, the idea of becoming vulnerable can be intimidating.

In my coaching practice, clients who've experienced multiple instances of sexual abuse often carry beliefs like "I am not safe," "I can't trust anyone," or "It's not safe to be me." Understandably, discussing these issues can be difficult for them. Before diving into details of the trauma or discussing the perpetrator, I find it most effective to first focus on establishing personal boundaries. This helps clients feel safe, empowered, and in control of their own bodies and decisions, laying the groundwork for trust in the coaching relationship.

Why dwell on the past, seeking justice or an apology, when you can focus on a happier life now? The perpetrator may not even remember you or what they did. Don't give power to painful memories. Our biology responds to our thoughts; if you can imagine a past hurt, you can also envision a positive future. By shifting your focus to thoughts and feelings that serve you, like "I am safe" instead of "I am not safe," you pave the way for healing and positive change. Changing your focus helps you create new neural pathways, leading to a healthier thought process.

Can an Analytical Mindset Shift to Embrace Emotions and Experience Transformation?

Looking at our problems logically can sometimes block us from engaging with the emotions and thoughts that shape our actions and behaviors. It's like reading a self-help book and grasping how to make

4. The Illusion of Safety: Revealing Hidden Benefits

positive changes but failing to feel these changes emotionally and comprehend the lessons at heart, which prevents actual change.

I read my first self-help book, *You Can Heal Your Life* by Louise Hay, at twenty-three. Three decades and five hundred books later, I realized that if I had taken the time to truly absorb and live by its teachings, it might have been the only guide I needed. I pursued self-development with an unhealed shadow, always wanting more without fully integrating what I had already learned, believing that more is better. I was living in my head and ego, not in my curious heart.

To cope with pain, some people use logic as a defense to block uncomfortable memories. In extreme cases, this could lead to dissociative disorders, which result in a disconnection from thoughts, memories, and surroundings. However, not everyone who turns to intellectualization is avoiding memories. Some may simply not be accustomed to expressing emotions, such as those from Asian cultures where there's a tradition of emotional restraint, influenced by cultural values that prioritize harmony and collective well-being.

Breathwork, yoga, sound baths, massages, and other relaxation techniques can enhance body awareness without requiring intense emotions or cathartic experiences. Simply relaxing and slowing our breath can be enough for meaningful change. When our nervous system unwinds, our bodies become more open to change. Acting in new directions, even without strong emotions, can still lead to positive shifts in our lives.

What Are the Shadows of Getting Stuck in Overprocessing Rather Than Healing?

Overprocessing can be a hindrance in our journey towards self-discovery and healing. Exploring different aspects of our being, including our emotions, psychology, and energy body, is crucial in uncovering the true self. It's like peeling the layers of a matryoshka doll where each layer reveals a new and hidden story about ourselves.

As we work through our challenges and negative thoughts, blocked emotions and energy may be released through means such as crying, shaking, or sudden realizations. This process can lead to new levels of consciousness and awareness, resulting in the release of endorphins, serotonin, and dopamine.

Discussing the same issues or individuals repeatedly can trigger a release of neurochemicals, making the cycle addictive. Our amygdala, the part of our brain responsible for emotions and for attaching significance to memories, can become conditioned to seek these neurochemical rewards. Some might indulge in endless emotional processing for the biochemical high, the bond felt during shared grievances, or as a way to sidestep personal responsibility under the guise of constant emotional turmoil.

While sharing feelings is essential for genuine relationships, incessantly focusing on our struggles can trap us in a loop of negativity. This can also pull others into a similar cycle if they get too enmeshed in our issues without seeking proactive solutions.

For lasting change, action is essential. While spirituality is important, we must also address our day-to-day responsibilities. Some might lean heavily on spiritual introspection as a way to avoid confronting real-world challenges, potentially due to a fear of taking on personal responsibility.

My mentor, Dr. Morris Netherton, used to say, "Some people are so heavenly, they're no earthly good." To truly align ourselves, we need to balance both realms by taking meaningful steps to improve our relationships, finances, and health.

Avoid getting stuck in a cycle of constantly seeking more, fearing change, or dodging conflict. This can lead to a false sense of progress and might not solve your core issues. True growth comes when we face our fears, acknowledge the need for change, and move beyond any

4. The Illusion of Safety: Revealing Hidden Benefits

barriers like secondary gains. Only then can we reap the benefits of our transformative journey.

How Being Future Outcome-Driven Keeps Us Stuck.

I worked with a woman who was married but in love with another man. Her marriage was lacking intimacy and connection and felt more like living with a roommate. Her husband was frugal with money and controlled her finances, rarely willing to go out or have fun. Despite her pleas for romance, he always cited saving money as the reason for his inaction.

The woman tried to get her husband to attend marriage counseling, but he refused. Instead, she joined a hiking group and met a man who she grew close to. She introduced him to her husband, who also became friends with him. After a year of spending time with this new man, she fell in love with him and told her husband. Her husband was taken aback and tried to make her feel guilty, but he was unaware of how the affair developed right in front of him.

Some of us have strong beliefs about how our lives and relationships will improve in the future. For example, we might say, "When I get the investors, my relationship with my wife will get better because my business will take off." Or we might believe that "If only he did this one thing" or "If only she were more punctual," our relationship would improve.

However, our relationships don't improve because we're not actively participating in what's needed in the present moment. It's like we're rearranging the furniture on the Titanic while the lifeboat is ready for us to jump in. When we create narratives about how our lives are "supposed to work" in the future, we're avoiding the issues and ignoring the potential solutions. Instead of taking responsibility and action in the present moment, we're putting our happiness on hold.

The archetypal energy of "waiting for our ships to come in," such as anticipating a big payday, can often be a way to avoid addressing underlying problems. We might believe that this financial windfall will resolve relationship issues or other challenges. Often, the secondary gain of focusing on future prospects is a diversion from deeper fears and insecurities. For instance, my client's husband felt like a failure due to financial setbacks and avoided discussing it with her. She simply wanted transparency and connection. By avoiding these conversations, he mistakenly believed that financial success would mend their relationship, all while sidestepping his own feelings of inadequacy.

Life continually provides feedback, whether it's conflicts with a spouse, job losses, friends distancing themselves, frequent minor accidents, health issues, or endless household repairs. This feedback is present in every moment, evident right before our eyes and within our bodies. Think of it like an alarm clock. If it goes off and we hit the *snooze* button only to oversleep and be late for work, the fault isn't with the clock. It's our responsibility to manage our time and sleep better.

Life isn't against us. Waiting for the *perfect moment* or for everything to align rarely works. Challenges, whether they involve relationships, household issues, or our emotions, arise in the present and need attention. The universe, our loved ones, and daily challenges all operate in the here and now. So, the real question is, are we ready to engage?

Will People I Love Be Okay if I Become Happy and Successful?

Santiago aspired to become a successful entrepreneur, but something always seemed to get in the way. He tried selling products, offering a service, and being part of a few startup companies, but none

4. The Illusion of Safety: Revealing Hidden Benefits

of them took off as he had hoped.

Whenever Santiago went out to a restaurant or was on vacation with his wife and children, he seemed unhappy and distracted. His wife told him, "Even if you had all the money in the world, I don't think you would be happy." This harsh truth was what prompted Santiago to seek coaching from me.

During our sessions, Santiago shared how guilty he felt for his siblings and mother who were not doing as well as he was. He said, "I feel so fucking guilty because my mother and siblings aren't doing well. It feels like I'm bragging about my great life while their lives are shit, but they're also negative about everything." As a result, Santiago downplayed his life with his family and avoided their phone calls.

Santiago told his mother he was away on business when he went on vacation, fearing her disapproval. His family, rooted in a poverty mentality, often criticized his ambitions, like when he left for college. His mother, with her negative views on wealth, seemed to believe her hardships were nobler than others' successes. As a result, Santiago believed he had to hide his true self to be accepted. His reluctance to confront his family stemmed from a fear of alienation and ongoing conflict. This avoidance represented a secondary gain from evading tough conversations. Thus, he developed the hidden belief, "If I avoid my truth, I'll remain part of this family."

If we grow up in an environment where we only witness hardship and struggle, we may develop the belief that life is inherently difficult and that things never work out. We may suppress our authentic feelings and say things like, "Things could be much worse, at least we have a roof over our head," or "We should be grateful for this food." These statements may be true, but we may be unconsciously avoiding conflict with loved ones, rather than taking personal responsibility and changing outdated family narratives that are no longer effective.

Perhaps our parents were immigrants who struggled to raise a family, or our ancestors experienced racism and other hardships that we no longer face. We may feel guilty, as if we owe them our suffering to maintain a sense of belonging. Instead of questioning and changing these family narratives, we may simply accept them.

Have you ever been told by a family member that all they wanted was for you to be happy? What if they didn't even know how to be happy themselves? How can our family members teach us happiness and success if all they were taught was how to survive? Perhaps you are the one who is meant to break the cycle of suffering by modeling happiness and thriving for the next generation. Maybe you are the family prophet and gift.

Will I Still Be Attractive and Receive Respect if I Lose My Social Status?

Frustrated clients have straight-out said, "I hate my job, and my boss is such an egotistical ass!" Nevertheless, the reason they don't just quit, voice their opinions, change departments, or find another job is because they believe their title is important, others are impressed by the company they work for, and for other reasons attached to social status.

Clients have climbed the corporate ladder only to find that it brings a tremendous amount of work and stress into their daily lives. Despite this, they hesitate to quit their jobs because they don't want to leave their wealthy neighborhoods, downsize their homes, give up their luxury cars, or move to a less expensive area. I have seen spouses remain in sexless, toxic relationships because their partner is well-respected, loved by their community, and has many friends. I once worked with a mechanic who was holding on to his failing family-owned mechanic shop, even though it hadn't made a profit in five years, because he was afraid of damaging the family's reputation.

Social constructs and status are influenced by our beliefs and hold no inherent value. When we're insecure, fearing others might not

4. The Illusion of Safety: Revealing Hidden Benefits

accept our true selves, we may maintain a false identity for perceived benefits, such as attention or respect for our achievements, appearance, or possessions. This *secondary gain* helps us evade confronting fears of failure, leading to hidden beliefs such as, "If they believe I'm succeeding, they'll respect me," or "If I keep smiling, I won't face vulnerable questions."

Shedding these false identities and beliefs is difficult, even if they bring stress, because we believe they're beneficial. Since social status is a construct, we aren't losing anything tangible. Yet, living inauthentically can be stifling. Our inner struggles arise from change, trust issues, and fear of the unknown. As our consciousness evolves, so do our desires, necessitating a life aligned with our growing awareness. Welcoming change is vital for soulful growth.

Releasing Secondary Gains Exercise

These questions will help uncover hidden beliefs that might create *secondary gains* limiting you. Even if you think you've identified the problem or know what triggers you, approach this exercise with an open mind to uncover potential underlying beliefs. Engage with every question, even if it seems irrelevant.

4. The Illusion of Safety: Revealing Hidden Benefits

To do this, read each question aloud, then silently to yourself, placing both hands over your heart. Allow the answers to flow, as if your heart is guiding the response. Document your insights.

Part One: Identifying Secondary Gains and Hidden Beliefs

If I were to change, communicate, forgive, or let go of _____ (person, situation), my greatest fears are _____.

The advantages of not changing, communicating, forgiving, or letting go of _____ (person, situation) are _____.

However, if I don't change, communicate, forgive, or let go, the disadvantages and challenges I might face in my life are _____.

If I were to be truly honest with myself, I'm afraid of _____.

I don't want to take responsibility for _____.

There's a part of me that doesn't want to change, communicate, forgive, or let go of _____ (person, situation) because _____.

Before I change, communicate, forgive, or let go of _____ (person, situation), I want them to know that I feel _____.

The reason I want them to know, and I feel this way is because _____.

If I were to change, communicate, forgive, or let go of _____ (person, situation), I don't want it to make me appear _____.

4. The Illusion of Safety: Revealing Hidden Benefits

I'm afraid of being seen as _____.

Part Two: Creating Your Future Self

We can't always predict the outcomes of our decisions, communications, or how others will respond to us. Regardless of external factors, it's our responsibility to decide the life we want to live and how we want to feel.

In the next part of the exercise, envision yourself filled with positivity, as if you've already overcome your challenges. Write as though you're living your best life now. This will help you craft an emotional blueprint for your ideal future self and energetically and emotionally align with your authentic self. It might also reveal hidden beliefs that are holding you back.

The sentence stems below are crafted to bring out and highlight the best in you, regardless of any limitations you might have placed on yourself. Fill in the blank, sharing about your future self, as if you can see, feel, hear, smell, taste, and connect to all the physical sensations in your body of your new future self.

Because I took personal responsibility for _____, the positive things I now tell myself are _____.

Now that I feel good and better, when I wake up in the morning and look in the mirror, I see _____.

By letting go of the stress and worrying about _____ (mention problem you were having), I'm now living my best life by _____.

Now that I feel more confidence and trust in myself and my decisions, the way my life has gotten better is by _____.

4. The Illusion of Safety: Revealing Hidden Benefits

I feel the best in my body and heart when I'm _____.

Every time I think of _____ I smile and feel good.

When I'm _____, it brings out the best in me.

Putting my attention on _____ helps me appreciate life and I feel gratitude.

Because I have a better demeanor and I look happier, when people see my smile, they say _____.

The happiest days of my life are when I'm _____.

After filling in the blanks, read these sentences as your new life script or affirmations to bolster the evolving version of yourself. If you're currently in a dilemma and considering a significant change in your life, read these sentences as often as needed to help you emotionally align with the changes you wish to experience in your life.

This exercise isn't about rash decisions, like suddenly quitting your job. Instead, it's designed to rise above any secondary gains that might be keeping you stuck, enhance clarity, empower you to live life on your terms, feel authentically yourself, and approach new challenges or adventures with confidence. If you've felt stuck or overly negative for a while, these affirmations can act like a torch in a dark cave, illuminating the joy and positivity in your life. They might just be the push you need to make the changes you've been contemplating.

5
Claiming Individual Power: Breaking Free from the Collective Script

When we resonate with the emotions of others, we feel a deep sense of connection and belonging. However, we must be aware of how these shared emotions influence us. While empathy is innate, it's crucial that we don't let others' negative perceptions or feelings overpower us or align our energy with theirs solely for connection. These energies can either elevate us or weigh us down, depending on the context.

When unexpected feelings of sadness, anger, or fear arise, it's worth considering the influence of collective consciousness. We are deeply interconnected, and global events, like the 2020 pandemic or political and climate shifts, resonate within our collective psyche. Such pronounced changes highlight the power of collective emotions: they can unite us during intense times, both in reality and in dreams. Yet, they might also introduce negativity, causing feelings like stress or pessimism, especially if we're facing personal challenges. As society's collective mindset shifts, it can induce chaos and uncertainty. When new ideas challenge our shared values, it leads to individual feelings of disorientation and confusion.

Imagine ourselves as a radio, with an antenna that picks up different stations. The quality of our physical health, emotional well-being, mindset, and presence determines how we'll channel and interpret the collective consciousness that surrounds us. Think of it as tidying up our emotional backyard so we can receive the most positive broadcasts. If we're under stress, using drugs or alcohol, eating poorly, or choosing to remain in a toxic relationship, we'll be more vulnerable and prone to interpreting information and collective energy in a fear-based way.

When unsettling events or information confront us, various factors could be at play. Our reactions might stem from personal empathy, past traumas, latent fears, or sometimes, we may not even understand why. Events like a celebrity's passing, a full moon, or a tragic incident might stir latent emotions, urging us to address and heal them. For instance, a woman with unresolved sexual trauma from a past assault might find a publicized trial more triggering. If financial worries burden us, the stock market's downturn might resonate more. Similarly, those feeling lonely might find the enthusiasm of those in relationships on Valentine's Day challenging. Often, our reactions to distressing news correlate with personal experiences. It's crucial to discern whether what we're feeling arises from our own issues, someone else's, the collective's worry, or is simply an unidentifiable emotion. Regardless, letting go of this unease can help ensure our well-being.

Addressing our emotional challenges enables us to access clearer, uplifting messages, fueling personal growth. By minimizing stress, limiting exposure to distressing news, connecting with positive individuals, and staying grounded, we can shield ourselves from negative collective influences. A consistent spiritual practice anchors us, fostering thoughtful decisions over impulsive ones. With heightened self-awareness and healing, we can truly "be in the world, not of it." This means that when grounded in our true selves and emotions, we can engage compassionately even in difficult times. Observing suffering or negativity doesn't have to disrupt our peace or relationships; instead, we can rise above, learn, keep our hearts open, and continue to contribute positively to humanity.

5. Claiming Individual Power: Breaking Free from the Collective Script

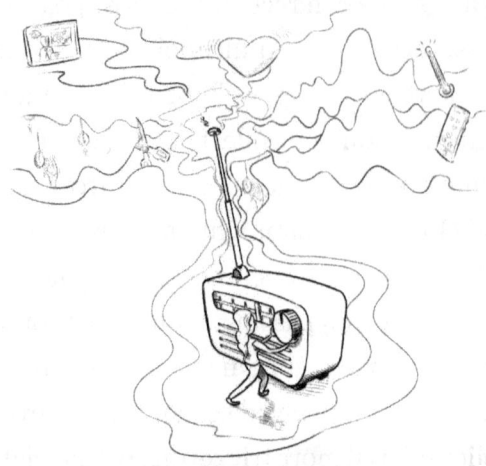

Cutting Free: Breaking the Chains of Collective Consciousness

The exercise you will undertake is designed to give you a deeper understanding of how the collective consciousness might be impacting your psyche and triggering you. By taking an emotional inventory and examining your relationship with the collective consciousness, you can discern the correlation between what's literally and personally going on in your life versus collective consciousness.

As your hidden beliefs and shadows become clearer and you release the tension surrounding them, the influence of the collective consciousness over you will diminish. You will gain the clarity to sever ties with anything that doesn't benefit you. While *cutting cords* might seem harsh or appear as a form of avoidance or indifference to some, it's not about that at all. Instead, it's about taking control of your mindset and emotions, so you aren't merely a puppet, unconsciously swayed by the collective consciousness. Instead of being subject to the world's fluctuations, you can choose to live life on your own terms.

1. To begin, find a quiet spot where you can sit undisturbed for a few minutes. If you're in a busy household or surrounded by

noise, no worries! You can head to the bathroom, take a quick shower, listen to calming music with headphones, or head to a park where you can connect with nature. All you need is five to ten minutes to complete this exercise.

2. Now, take a moment to *think* about what's been causing you negative feelings lately. Maybe it's something you saw on the news, heard at work, read on social media, or even discussed with a friend. It's important to be honest with yourself and allow any feelings, judgments, or fears to arise without suppressing them. You see, there's always a connection between what's happening in the world and our personal lives. By acknowledging our negative thoughts, we can gain greater control over our emotions and prevent them from taking over our lives.

3. As you focus on the emotions that arise from thinking about the negative story, such as what you saw on the news, what you heard in the elevator, what people around you keep talking about, the article in the morning newspaper, the earthquake that killed thousands of people, the stock market report, or the car accident you passed on the freeway, allow yourself to hold the story in your mind as if you're a journalist reporting the news from a conscious and emotional space of neutrality. Take a step back and observe the story without judgment, neither identifying with it nor rejecting it. Answer the following questions:

I feel _____ about _____ (problem/situation).

The core emotions and thoughts I feel about _____ are _____.

These feelings directly impact my personal life because _____.

5. Claiming Individual Power: Breaking Free from the Collective Script

The problem/situation outside of me stirs up emotions within me because _____.

I wish I could feel _____ instead of _____.

Examples include:

- I'm devastated about the earthquake, feeling terrible for those who have died or are now homeless. My own safety and well-being are also a concern. I don't feel safe in my relationship with my boyfriend and its direction. I wish I could feel more independent and less worried about what he's doing.
- The coaching industry worries me. It seems like inexperienced coaches are saturating the field, and I'm unsure if my coaching business will succeed. The thought of having to get a regular job is unsettling. I wish I could feel more confident in my abilities to succeed in coaching.
- I don't trust the government—I feel they're lying to us and taking away our freedom to make our own choices. Trust issues are present in many areas of my life. I wish I could feel more supported, so I can improve my life.
- Why don't others take their health more seriously? I fear that I may not have a strong immune system and I could die. Perhaps, it's not death itself that I fear, but the idea that I haven't accomplished all that I wanted to in life. I wish I had more clarity about my purpose instead of feeling so much uncertainty.
- I get very jealous when I see others being more successful than me. At forty-five years old, I feel like all my friends are ahead of me and it makes me feel like a loser. I wish I had more confidence in myself and stopped comparing myself to others.

The last sentence in the exercise, "I wish I could feel _____ instead of _____," emphasizes focusing on desired feelings

5. Claiming Individual Power: Breaking Free from the Collective Script

rather than undesired ones. All preceding questions guide you to comprehend your emotions, identify how you want to feel, and transition from any feelings of hopelessness or lack of awareness about your surroundings.

For example, during the initial months of the 2020 pandemic, I was inundated with couples seeking guidance due to relationship strains. Most realized that the prolonged togetherness during the mandates and lockdowns intensified pre-existing issues. The societal uncertainty we all faced seemed to magnify hidden concerns and unresolved disputes. It was being thrown into a metaphorical sweat lodge, where the continuous friction and disputes brought concealed issues into sharp focus. Their usual distractions, like late work hours or evenings at the bar, had previously allowed them to avoid confronting these relationship challenges. The lockdowns, however, illuminated what was left unhealed.

On the other hand, there were individuals actively engaged in introspection and self-improvement during this period. They took up online yoga, sought coaching via Zoom, and communicated openly and responsibly about their concerns. These individuals understood that their anxiety was internal, not just a reaction to external events or societal unrest. Despite facing the same challenges as everyone else, they stayed grounded, compassionate, and committed to their spiritual journeys. Some, including myself, used the time to complete long-postponed tasks like fixing a fence or decluttering a garage—letting go of old attachments. I built a homemade sauna to detox and catch up on my reading. This isn't about one method being better but noticing how differently we all cope under the same pressures. In times of chaos, it's crucial to remain grounded, transcend collective narratives, and connect with our higher selves.

When we remain heart-centered, firmly grounded to the earth while keeping our consciousness attuned to the heavens, we better support those in pain. Think of Mother Teresa, constantly surrounded by the sick and suffering. Had she been easily emotionally triggered, could she have been the beacon of light that she was? If she lacked the ability to distinguish others' despair from her own emotions, she couldn't have fostered faith, hope, love, or a connection to God. Consider Amma, the hugging saint, who goes without rest for days, embracing over five-thousand people burdened with immense pain. Most might absorb that energy, especially when confronted with someone grieving a child's death or appearing close to their own end.

I'm not implying one must attain a saint-like detachment, but through prayer, positive affirmations, meditation in nature for global peace, or volunteering, you can make a difference. By addressing our hidden beliefs and somewhat distancing ourselves from the collective pain, we can better create a healing space for the world's suffering. We all possess the potential to be Earth's guardians and angels.

6
Rising Above Myths: Unleashing the Inner Hero

The journey of healing and growth is continuous and ever-evolving. While we may reach milestones like healing from trauma or achieving sobriety, life always presents new challenges and opportunities for development. True happiness and self-fulfillment aren't destinations but ongoing journeys.

Growing emotionally, intellectually, and spiritually is a profound journey. Delving into our depths to heal and evolve is both challenging and rewarding. This path demands personal responsibility; no one else can undertake it for us. While the uncertainty and responsibility of this journey can be daunting, those who accept the challenge find transformative rewards.

Throughout history, tales of heroes on quests for greatness and personal growth have resonated across cultures. These stories of self-discovery and healing underscore the essence of human experience. Rooted in our collective consciousness, the hero's journey reflects our shared struggles and triumphs.

As we evolve, we arm ourselves with tools for a more genuine life. We learn to set boundaries, trust our intuition, and build inner confidence, allowing us to navigate future challenges with greater ease and assurance.

According to American writer and philosopher Joseph Campbell, our personal journey often starts with self-improvement, progresses to aiding our family, and ultimately leads to contributing to the community. Our aim is to enhance our self-awareness, promote prosperity and health, uplift humanity, create resources and connections, and share our newfound wisdom either by teaching or by exemplifying our awakenings and transformations.

The Hero's Journey, according to Joseph Campbell, has twelve steps:

1. **Ordinary World:** Showing the hero's normal life before the adventure.
2. **Call to Adventure:** The hero is challenged to start their journey.
3. **Refusal of the Call:** The hero may initially hesitate or be afraid.
4. **Meeting the Mentor:** A guide helps the hero prepare for their journey.
5. **Crossing the Threshold:** The hero leaves their familiar world for the first time.
6. **Tests, Allies, and Enemies:** The hero faces challenges, makes friends, and meets enemies in their new world.
7. **The Approach:** The hero tries to solve the main conflict but faces obstacles.
8. **The Ordeal:** The hero goes through difficult challenges and a crisis.
9. **The Reward:** The hero earns a reward after overcoming challenges.
10. **The Road Back:** The hero is close to the end but still faces challenges.
11. **The Resurrection:** The hero faces the final test and solves the conflict.
12. **The Return:** The hero brings the solution back to their ordinary world.

6. Rising Above Myths: Unleashing the Inner Hero

The journey of the human spirit possesses boundless potential and transformative power. The archetypes guiding us on this journey aren't confined to a specific type of person. Instead, they are fluid and adaptable, shaping themselves to meet individual needs. Each of us follows a unique spiritual curriculum, but our human experiences might share similarities. By understanding our consciousness and our role in life, we can enhance our lives and transcend the limitations of a constrained existence.

When stressed or not fully grounded in our bodies, it's natural for us to act, feel, and think negatively. This is exacerbated when we aren't living authentically, neglect self-care, or face several challenges at once. For example, during my father's health decline amid the 2020 pandemic, I learned of my son's retained primitive reflexes that were negatively impacting his ability to learn to read, and securing an in-person tutor became difficult due to the prevailing uncertainties.

This stress caused me to display darker aspects of the archetypal king and caregiver. I became controlling, raised my voice, and felt unsupported. My energy was depleted, and resentment grew as my personal goals took a backseat, leading to passive-aggressive behavior. However, when I found an outdoor workout spot, I felt rejuvenated and more present, allowing me to be more patient with my son and the challenges we encountered.

It's crucial to understand that none of us are alone in our highs and lows. Intriguingly, our interconnected consciousness and energy result in our embodying various shades of archetypes. Recognizing these archetypes highlights the underlying hidden beliefs and behaviors we unconsciously adopt, often from childhood or media influences.

Often, we are drawn to personalities, including how they handle stress, especially those we admire or see frequently, such as our parents. Films and plays introduce us to archetypal characters like the

6. Rising Above Myths: Unleashing the Inner Hero

villain, hero, or teacher, each with distinct motivations. We all navigate our life stories, aspiring to be its hero. Sometimes, we resonate with characters for reasons unknown, like my affinity for Harrison Ford's character, Indiana Jones, during my teenage years because of his intelligence, bravery, integrity, and, as a teenage boy, his appeal to women.

There are hidden beliefs that influence why we are attracted to and identify with certain archetypal characters. For example, if we felt victimized, abandoned, or were raised in foster care, we might gravitate towards the orphan archetype, as exemplified by characters like Batman or Emma Stone's role in the movie *Cruella*.

I've outlined eighteen prevalent archetypes in modern culture that may align with your personality traits, whether you're feeling positive or negative. Explore these archetypes, considering their character traits, attitudes, demeanor, emotions, and behaviors. Trust your intuition and focus on the archetypes that immediately captivate you. They might unveil *hidden beliefs* and offer insights that help you understand yourself more deeply, unlocking your full human potential. Remember, it's possible to resonate with multiple archetypes.

The Eighteen Human Collective Archetypes

1. The Caregiver: The Motherly Archetype

The Caregiver, previously known as the Mother, is an archetype who gives wholeheartedly and selflessly to those around them, often at their own expense. This archetype can be a parent, best friend, partner, teacher, mentor, guardian, sibling, and more.

While the Caregiver may not be in the spotlight, they support others and encourage them to give their all. They are often viewed as the selfless companion to the person striving to become a hero.

The Light: Compassionate, loving, unconditional, caring, selfless, loyal, honorable, reliable, and consistent.

The Shadow: Over-selflessness, people-pleasing tendencies, vulnerability from giving too much, lack of personal goals or growth. They may become passive-aggressive when they feel they are giving too much or when their expectations are not met.

Examples: Mother Teresa, Tara, Quan Yin, Mary Poppins, Hagrid from *Harry Potter*, Samwise Gamgee from *The Lord of the Rings*, and Charlotte from *Charlotte's Web*.

2. The Regular Guy: The Relatable Person Archetype

The Regular archetype is someone to whom many can easily relate. They are the hardworking individuals who embody the spirit of the *salt of the earth*. Despite a lack of higher education or experiences beyond their daily life, they possess a depth of understanding and knowledge.

The Regular archetype values security over grandeur and is approachable, making it effortless for others to connect with them. However, they may struggle to distinguish themselves and can blend into the background.

6. Rising Above Myths: Unleashing the Inner Hero

The Light: Empathetic, hardworking, kind, virtuous, accepting, a sense of belonging, grounded, relatable, down-to-earth, friendly, and simple.

The Shadow: Powerlessness, perfectionist, boredom, loneliness, black-and-white thinking, uniqueness, purposeless, passionless, unpreparedness, a tendency to go with the flow too often, conflict avoidance, and a tendency to be either too passive or passive-aggressive.

Examples: Bilbo Baggins from *The Lord of the Rings*, Ron Weasley from *Harry Potter*, Anastasia from *Anastasia*, Leslie Knope from *Parks and Recreation*, Ryan Reynolds in *Free Guy*, and Emmet Brickowski from *The Lego Movie*.

3. The Innocent/Child: The Naive and Optimistic Archetype

The Innocent, often depicted as a child or child-like, possesses boundless optimism and naivety. Their actions and intentions are morally pure, starting from a good and comfortable place until an event transforms their world, revealing a reality that was previously ignored or had no impact on them.

The Light: Honest, trusting, enthusiastic, compassionate, loving, sincere, kind, always smiling, joyful, sees the world through innocence.

The Shadow: Naive, overly trusting, powerless, unaware, inexperienced, vulnerable to harm, lacks personal responsibility, afraid to speak up, feels unseen, a lack of authenticity can lead to sadness behind their smile.

Examples: Scout from *To Kill a Mockingbird*, Merry and Pippen from *The Lord of the Rings*, and Rapunzel from *Tangled*.

4. The Jester or Comedian: The Lighthearted Archetype

The Joker or Jester archetype is a character who brings humor and joy to a story. They live in the moment, are independent, and often provide comic relief. This archetype is not bound by the primary goal of the hero, but instead adds their unique perspective and lightheartedness to the narrative.

The Light: Fun-loving, humorous, charming, insightful, reminding us to embrace our individuality and bring humor and joy to our lives.

The Dark: Superficial, impulsive, using humor to deflect, avoiding responsibility, and potentially appearing insensitive through gratuitous humor.

Examples: Harley Quinn from *Suicide Squad*, R2D2 and C-3PO from *Star Wars*, Dory from *Finding Nemo*, Vince Vaughn in *Swingers*, Bill Murray in *Stripes*, and comedian Russell Brand.

5. The Ruler or King: The Authority Archetype

The Ruler holds authority, either through legal, emotional, or military means and is responsible for others. They can either rule with an iron fist for their own benefit or be viewed as a compassionate and selfless leader.

The greatest fear for a Ruler is a threat to their control, which can result in the loss of power and harm to those they are protecting. If insecure or stressed, the Ruler may resort to domination through force and intimidation. At the root of their need to control others is a desire to control their emotions, environment, and to hide their vulnerability.

The Light: The Ruler is powerful, stable, holds a high status, has access to resources, is charismatic, decisive, courageous, objective, well-connected, politically intelligent, and natural leader who understands the dynamics of people and power.

The Dark: The Ruler can also be controlling, out of touch, disliked, have many enemies, be greedy, fear losing their position, and feel weak. If they are disconnected from their heart, they may become a villainous Ruler motivated solely by greed, which can become quickly boring.

Conversely, a benevolent Ruler who knows everything can become too predictable.

The levels of the Ruler archetype can include taking responsibility for one's own life, leading a family or group, and holding a higher level of leadership within the community or government.

Examples: Mufasa from *The Lion King*, King Arthur, Dr. Martin Luther King Jr., Mahatma Gandhi, Richard Branson, Nelson Mandela, and Winston Churchill.

6. The Sage: The Spiritual Guru Archetype

The Sage archetype, also known as the mentor, shaman, or spiritual teacher, shares some similarities with the Magician archetype. However, while the Magician seeks to advance themselves, the Sage seeks to assist others. Possessing vast knowledge, skills, and life experiences, the Sage may have been mentored by a teacher and now devotes their life's purpose and passion to passing on this wisdom to their pupils. As a guide and a source of inspiration, the Sage helps others navigate life's challenges and discover their own path towards personal growth and enlightenment.

The Light: Wise, logical, loving, humble, compassionate, rational, relatable, caring, patient, insightful, and a source of guidance and support.

The Dark: Dogmatic, critical of their students, cold, arrogant, self-righteous, isolated, pompous, self-important, and frustratingly vague or cryptic with their teachings.

Examples: Gandalf from *The Lord of the Rings*, Professor Dumbledore from *Harry Potter*, The Oracle from *The Matrix*, Obi-

Wan Kenobi from *Star Wars*, Jackie Chan in *The Karate Kid*, and Master Oogway from *Kung Fu Panda*.

7. The Lover: The Romantic Archetype

The Lover is guided by their heart and emotions, ranging from hopeless romantics to playboys. They will often change or sacrifice themselves in pursuit of acquiring or maintaining love, viewing the object of their affection as the most important thing in their life, much like the Creator and their creation.

The Light: Devoted, compassionate, caring, protective, romantic, selfless, and driven by love, the Lover values beauty in the world and is motivated to attract it. They are good at receiving love, foster bliss and unity, and are passionate.

The Dark: The Lover can become overly dramatic, shallow, obsessed, prone to sacrificing themselves, scared of loneliness, prone to jealousy, and lack a strong sense of self. They can become consumed by their emotions.

Examples: Belle from **Beauty and the Beast**, Luna Lovegood from *Harry Potter*, Romeo and Juliet, Edward Cullen from *Twilight*, Bridget Jones from *Bridget Jones's Diary,* and Princess Anna from *Frozen*.

8. The Creator: The Creative Archetype

The Creator finds happiness in the act of creation and is often consumed by a single project that they are working towards. They are driven to push boundaries and leave a lasting impact. Their creations can be tangible, such as those of an inventor, entrepreneur, musician, or artist. To the Creator, nothing is more important than their creation, and they are willing to make sacrifices, including themselves and others, to achieve their goal. Their self-identity, purpose, and joy are in their creation or project.

6. Rising Above Myths: Unleashing the Inner Hero

The Light: Imaginative, innovative, ambitious, creative, driven, strong-willed, non-conforming, solution-oriented, and fun-loving.

The Shadow: Single-minded, obsessive, perfectionist, selfish, ungrounded, unreliable, egotistical, eccentric, unrelatable, and prone to making sacrifices, including those that could be irresponsible towards family or their job.

Examples: Gene Wilder in *Willy Wonka & the Chocolate Factory*, Robert Downey Jr. in *Iron Man*, Dick Van Dyke in *Chitty Chitty Bang Bang*, Christopher Lloyd in *Back to the Future*, and Albert Einstein.

9. The Explorer: The Adventurous Archetype

The Explorer is a restless individual who seeks adventure and excitement beyond the boundaries of their daily life. They are unsatisfied with the status quo and feel confined by societal norms, seeking new experiences, knowledge, and personal growth. This could be a person who lives a nomadic lifestyle, traveling and working remotely.

The Light: Bravery, determination, ambition, independence, non-conformity, drive, curiosity, adventure, daring, and a pride in their individuality.

The Shadow: Never-ending dissatisfaction, easily bored, a lack of direction, impulsiveness, social isolation, self-centeredness, indifference to the consequences of their actions; and a fear of settling down, taking responsibility, creating stability in their life, and trusting their decisions.

Examples: Harrison Ford in *Indiana Jones*, Jennifer Lawrence in *The Hunger Games*, and Bilbo Baggins in *The Lord of the Rings*.

10. The Orphan: The Abandoned Archetype

The Orphan is an archetype who is taken from a state of insignificance or poverty and thrown into a world of excitement or grandeur. They are in search of a sense of belonging and a surrogate family to replace the one they never had or lost.

The Light: Survivalist, empathetic, determined, driven, resilient, resourceful, compassionate, forgiving, adaptable, supportive of the underdog, and willing to fight for a cause to help others.

The Shadow: Scarcity of resources, "I must do it all alone" attitude, distrust, lack of confidence, naïveté, vulnerability, manipulability, victim mentality, feeling like an outsider, apathy, and absence of personal responsibility.

Examples: Oliver Twist, Bruce Wayne from *Batman*, Aladdin, Tarzan, Keanu Reeves in *The Matrix*, Chris Pratt in *Guardians of the Galaxy*, and Jennifer Lawrence in *The Hunger Games*.

11. The Hero: The Brave Archetype

The Hero is an archetype that embodies courage and resilience in the face of challenges. They can be a reluctant hero, who is initially resistant to their newfound role, or someone who is confronted with an injustice and must push through it. They may also be a person struggling with their own psychological battles, seeking happiness on the other side.

The Light: Strength, persistence, emotional resilience, courage, honor, a strong sense of right and wrong, compassion, selflessness, and a commitment to a cause. They stand up for the underdog and serve as a role model to others.

The Shadow: Arrogance, hubris, blind faith, insensitivity to others, an ego-driven nature, and a tendency to ignore the consequences of their actions. They may also have a *lone wolf* complex and struggle to acknowledge their own limitations.

Examples: Superman, Wonder Woman, Luke Skywalker from *Star*

Wars, Jennifer Lawrence in *The Hunger Games*, and Buffy the Vampire Slayer.

12. The Outlaw/Rebel: The Antagonistic Archetype

The Outlaw or Rebel archetype rises to challenge broken leaders and flawed power structures. These characters are unapologetically themselves and inspire others to join their cause. They may be the public face of a rebellion, a charismatic outsider, or someone who exposes the shadows of outdated, crooked, or misunderstood systems. The Outlaw desires change and will stop at nothing to achieve it, serving as a disruptive force that aims to shake up the status quo, whether for selfish reasons or to improve the lives of others.

The Light: Natural leader, independent, courageous, inspiring, strong, charismatic, virtuous, and resourceful.

The Shadow: Obsessive, misguided anger, impulsiveness, excessive stress, uncompromising behavior, a lack of resources and means of power, breaks the law, or becoming fanatical.

Examples: Robin Hood, Harrison Ford in *Star Wars*, Jennifer Lawrence in *The Hunger Games*, and Ariel from *The Little Mermaid*.

13. The Seductress: The Seductive Archetype

The Seductress is an archetype that embodies the allure of power and the dangers of ambition. This character, who may be male or female, uses their wit, intellect, physicality, or leverage to achieve their goals, often at the expense of others. They are known for making promises that come with strings attached, offering something of value, but the trade-off always benefits them more than what they are giving up. The Seductress archetype is not limited by gender, sex, age, motive, or means and can utilize various avenues of power (political, economic, magical, etc.) to get what they want.

6. Rising Above Myths: Unleashing the Inner Hero

The Light: Charismatic, playful, sensual, passionate, resourceful, fiercely independent, healthy sexual energy, intelligent, clever, witty.

The Shadow: Manipulative, unapologetic behavior, selfish, standoffish, tendency towards greed, obsession with artificial power, arrogant, fear of vulnerability and commitment.

Examples: Puss in Boots, Kim Cattrall in *Sex and the City*, Black Widow from the Marvel Universe, Mystique from *X-Men*, Jessica Rabbit from *Who Framed Roger Rabbit,* the rockstar or playboy type of man, the Sirens from ancient Greece, and Mephistopheles from the tale of Faust.

14. The Magician: The Power and Skill Archetype

The Magician archetype can be found in both heroes and villains. They're known for their extraordinary skills and abilities, which can sometimes seem inhuman. Unlike the Hero, who may seek power to help others, the Magician is often driven by a desire for more power for themselves. It is important to note that power, in this context, can refer to various forms of influence, including knowledge, political capital, wealth, physical or mental strength, etc.

The Light: Intelligent, wise, powerful, disciplined, clever, omnipotent, intuitive, perceptive.

The Shadow: Arrogant, hubris, selfish, obsessive, indifferent.

Examples: Emma Watson in *Harry Potter*, Doctor Strange from the Marvel Universe, Rachel McAdams in *Mean Girls*, Sherlock Holmes, and Gandalf from *The Lord of the Rings*.

15. Peter Pan: The Forever-Child Archetype

The Peter Pan archetype embodies the enthusiastic, passionate, and youthful spirit that may be attractive to others but may not make for a reliable partner. This person may resist taking personal responsibility, growing up, and performing mundane tasks such as paying bills. They can be unreliable, avoid commitment, and struggle with getting things done. The routine aspects of life may bore them.

Even as adults, their parents may still be taking care of them, and their lovers, friends, or parents may constantly rescue them by paying their bills, providing them with a place to stay, or supporting their fun and travels.

The Light: Enthusiastic, adventurous, playful, joyful, sensual, romantic, creative, communicative, fearless, hopeful, optimistic, imaginative.

The Shadow: Self-centered, oblivious, carefree, boastful, arrogant, forgetful, inability to grow up and take on responsibilities.

Examples: Peter Pan, Simba from *The Lion King*, Seth Rogen in *Knocked Up*, Greta Gerwig in *Frances Ha*, Paul Rudd in *This is 40*, Ed Westwick in *Gossip Girl*, and Charlize Theron in *Young Adult*.

16. The Pessimist: The Disenchanted Archetype

The Pessimist archetype highlights the bleakest aspects of life, preparing for the most unfavorable outcomes—essentially, the glass half-empty perspective. Individuals who embody this archetype often lack hope and joy, their worldview tainted by skepticism and mistrust. In essence, pessimists expect the worst in every situation, transitioning from a sense of being misunderstood to harboring resentment. Students entrenched in this archetype anticipate demanding exams and disheartening grades, while workers foresee impending layoffs. Similarly, job applicants predict rejection during the interview process.

The Pessimist archetype contends with the apprehension of confronting adversity and tribulation. Molded by past or present

6. Rising Above Myths: Unleashing the Inner Hero

emotional traumas, those who personify this archetype may indeed be victims of their circumstances. Yet, they frequently perceive hardships as insurmountable obstacles rather than opportunities for growth.

The Light: Discerning, meticulous, stable, reliable, and consistent.

The Shadow: Self-absorbed, embittered, despondent, purposeless, hopeless, doubtful, clinging to the past, expecting the worst, blameful, and shirking responsibility.

Examples: Tom Hanks in *Otto*, Carroll O'Connor in *All in the Family*, Carl Fredricksen from *Up*, Clint Eastwood in *Gran Torino*, Eeyore in *Winnie-the-Pooh*, and Kurtwood Smith in *That '70s Show*.

17. The Consumer: The Consumer Archetype

The Consumer archetype is characterized by individuals whose lives center around social media, the pursuit of aesthetic perfection, and acquiring the latest material possessions. They are often captivated by television and entangled in the latest news and gossip. However, these individuals frequently assimilate information without exercising discernment, self-awareness, or conducting independent research.

Lacking a strong sense of self and incongruous character traits, those embodying the Consumer archetype allow themselves to be molded by the influence of social media, television, film, and the collective consciousness. Their worth becomes contingent on conforming to external validation, leading to an estrangement from their unique essence.

Instead of pursuing education, addressing insecurities through therapy, embracing personal responsibility, or navigating life's challenges in a healthy manner, they may depend on superficial factors such as physical appearance, social status, romantic partners, vehicles, social circles, and follower counts. Their self-concept and purpose become codependent on the opinions and emotions of others, leaving them vulnerable to external influences.

The Light: Curious, funny, attractive, interest in others, influential, lighthearted.

The Shadow: Shallow, superficial, lack substance and depth, insecure, gullible, have a constant need for validation and approval, lack boundaries, and sexual energy.

Examples: Kim Kardashian, Paris Hilton, Instagram models, Alicia Silverstone in *Clueless*, Rachel McAdams in *Mean Girls*, and Aubrey Plaza in *Ingrid Goes West*.

18. The People-Pleaser: The "Let's Make Everyone Happy" Archetype

The People-Pleasing archetype prioritizes keeping others happy, often at their own expense. They avoid conflict and neglect their own needs. They act as cheerleaders, remaining loyal to those who mistreat them in the hope that they will one day appreciate them. People-pleasers can become martyrs, sacrificing themselves for others' benefit without realizing the harm they're causing themselves. Women who sacrifice their own lives to save their relationships often embody this archetype.

Rescuers are also part of this archetype, deriving value from helping others in distress. However, this can lead to the end of the relationship once the person no longer needs help. It's important for people pleasers to recognize their own needs and boundaries to truly help others.

The Light: Kind, caring, loyal, a good listener, helpful, empathetic, supportive, reliable, a great giver, and always ready to help those in need.

The Shadow: Avoids conflict, inauthentic, hides their true motive, can be easily manipulated and exploited, mental and emotional exhaustion, not good at receiving help from others.

Examples: Lily James in *Yesterday*, Kristen Schaal in *The Boss*, and Jenna Fischer in *Blades of Glory*.

Creating Your Hero's Journey Vision Board

Exploring archetypes offers a fascinating lens to view our behavioral patterns and understand if they're manifesting constructively or destructively. For instance, one might embrace the Rebel archetype in response to perceived injustices, but this can lead to becoming consumed by the cause, causing tension in other areas of life. Maybe you identified with the Seductress in your youth, using charm to achieve your desires. However, as you transitioned into your fifties and parenthood, the Caregiver archetype dominated, and you now yearn to rediscover that allure, albeit with deeper wisdom.

Embracing our authentic selves without barriers allows for greater adaptability in our behaviors. Just as actors immerse themselves into diverse roles, capturing each character's unique emotions and quirks, we too can adapt different facets of our personality. This isn't about mere *acting* but genuinely embodying the essence of an archetype or, even better, the finest versions of ourselves.

In essence, if years of harboring resentment and anger have shaped you, it's vital to reflect on your current self and decide who you aspire to be. Recognizing specific archetypes can illuminate both your strengths and weaknesses. If drawn to a certain archetype, focus on its positive attributes. Delving into shadow work reveals hidden beliefs that might drive the more negative behaviors associated with your archetypal persona. Moreover, understanding the tangible presence of archetypal energy in our society makes it easier to avoid being trapped in detrimental patterns.

6. Rising Above Myths: Unleashing the Inner Hero

After exploring the different archetypes and identifying with one or more of them, read their specific character traits, including their lighter and darker aspects. Then, take a pause for at least five minutes, connecting to your heart and breath. Afterward, answer the following questions on your computer, phone, or a piece of paper.

1. **Archetype identification** - What is your archetype, and how do its lighter and darker aspects manifest in relation to the problem you're addressing?

   What is your archetype, and how do its lighter and darker aspects manifest in relation to the problem you're addressing?

2. **Problem recognition** - What issues and emotions in your life trigger the darker aspects of the archetypal character you resonate with?

3. **Emotional and behavioral impact** - How does the problem affect your emotions, behavior, and actions?

4. **Current stage of the hero's journey** - What steps are you taking to tackle the problem? Do you feel you're at the beginning, middle, or end of your journey to overcome this issue?

5. **Envisioning the inner hero** - If the problem were resolved, how would your actions and emotions change?

6. **Aspiring to feel like the inner hero** - Picture the best version of yourself, exuding confidence and positivity. What would alter in your life?

7. **Supporting your hero's journey** - What daily habits, support, and resources can help you become your life's hero, directing your emotions and actions to enhance your strengths, and overcome your weaknesses? Consider affirmations, meditation, exercise, nature walks, reducing alcohol, eating healthy, finding an accountability partner, coaching, cutting off toxic relationships, better sleep habits, and embracing positive aspects while conquering negative traits.

Next, you'll craft a powerful vision board that captures the positive qualities of your archetype, combined with the strengths of other archetypes. Imagine receiving superpowers from various Marvel heroes to support you on your hero's journey.

Your Hero's Journey Vision Board should be a collage of visual images and words that depict the life you desire, the positive traits you aim to embody, and the best version of yourself taking decisive actions to enhance your life. This vision board stands as a tangible symbol of your aspirations in life and relationships. These images and words will assist you in actualizing your goals and vision.

You can assemble a physical vision board using pictures cut from magazines, printed images from the internet glued onto an 11x17 paper or cardboard. Alternatively, you can design a digital version to display on your desktop or phone. Visit *raydoktor.com/exercises* for visual samples.

Vision boards are profoundly effective. They serve as a continuous visual reminder of your optimal self and the objectives you aspire to, such as a tranquil monk atop a mountain with cascading waterfalls symbolizing calmness and self-care; a man confidently presenting to prospective clients during a meeting; an individual overcoming a health challenge while jogging on a beach; someone relishing camping moments with their family, signifying treasured leisure; a woman enjoying wine with friends to convey connection; a warrior conquering demons as a representation of defeating cancer; a deer, signifying gentle communication; or a couple nestled by a fire, exemplifying the love and wholesome relationship you hope to welcome into your life.

Remember, many of us are drawn to inspirational movies based on true stories and real-life experiences. Deep within, we find reflections of our own stories in these cinematic journeys—our hidden fears, looming challenges, and the boundless horizon of what could be once we embrace our truths. Yet, most people remain spectators,

6. Rising Above Myths: Unleashing the Inner Hero

watching others achieve their goals, perform passionately, regain their health, complete their education, leave unhealthy relationships, or reconnect with estranged family members. In movies, these moments are heightened with stirring soundtracks and heart-touching scripts. However, our daily lives can be just as profound when we are fully present and authentic. Even the smallest necessary change in your life sends positive ripples across the cosmic sea. Each step you take towards betterment not only uplifts you but also inspires others. We all have the potential to illuminate the world.

7
Vital Vortexes: Activating Your Energy Anatomy

Minor alterations in our environment can significantly influence our energy system. Our diet, exercise habits, relationships, media consumption, sleep patterns, illnesses, workspaces, living locations, and even shared societal energies all play a role. These elements shape our mood, physical health, and our connections to ourselves and others.

It's easy to overlook or downplay negative sensations in our bodies and relationships, especially if things seem fine externally or to the outside world. However, when we ignore these signals, they can amplify over time, compelling us to address them. The core of the issue may not be immediately apparent, but it can manifest as bodily tension or unexpected events such as a car accident, a plumbing problem in our bathroom, our nanny quitting without notice, or troubling individuals from our past suddenly reappearing in our lives.

Occasionally, our energy can become stagnant. It's not necessary to pinpoint the exact source of this stagnation or the underlying hidden belief. In our evolving journey of consciousness, we might not discern every adverse impact on us. However, when dense energy builds up in our system, we may feel confined, unable to move forward. For instance, while establishing my co-parenting relationship, I held back certain thoughts to avoid conflict and ensure smooth communication

7. Vital Vortexes: Activating Your Energy Anatomy

for my son's sake. This restraint, however, caused a lingering mild throat discomfort due to blocked energy. To be better prepared for coaching or speaking engagements, and to ensure my throat is open and I'm speaking authentically from my heart, I perform a throat chakra-clearing exercise.

In my coaching program and retreats, I incorporate chakra clearing and rebalancing, especially when clients face prolonged challenges or physical trauma. For instance, someone fresh out of a relationship and looking to date might still harbor lingering energy from a painful breakup. This could explain their pattern of attracting unavailable partners; they might be clinging to past hurt or shielding themselves to avoid future pain.

When the root chakra is misaligned, one might find themselves drawn to unstable partners. Likewise, lingering sexual trauma can lead to connections with highly sexual or emotionally abusive partners. An imbalanced chakra often draws in discordant and unhealthy experiences. The state of our relationships often reflects the openness or closure of our chakras. Chronic closure of chakras doesn't stem from fleeting stress but from prolonged strains like financial troubles, caregiving for a seriously ill loved one, enduring toxic relationships, or staying in an unfulfilling job. Over time, our bodies accumulate *crud* from inauthentic living, negativity, unhealthy habits, and stagnation.

Understanding the chakra system provides insights into our emotional, mental, and physical well-being. By tuning into these energy centers, we can identify imbalances, particularly those arising from hidden beliefs. If we've been trapped in a behavioral pattern, balancing our chakra might require more attention. However, for day-to-day experiences that contract our energy, merely listening to a comedian on the radio can make us burst into laughter, receiving a tantalizing picture from our beloved, or deeply savoring the aroma of our coffee can effortlessly open up our entire body and heart, aligning our chakras.

There are times when words cannot capture our fears, when no memories or stories relate to our pain, or when the cause of our feelings of being stuck remains elusive. Sometimes, blocked energy is simply stagnant, and we don't need to understand why. The unconscious mind occasionally provides us with cognitive impressions and images, and at times it's accessed through the body, as if the body contains hidden cellular memory.

By releasing energy from a chakra, we might suddenly recall an event or experience an intense cathartic purge, like a former female client of mine who sought coaching after a therapeutic massage. When the female massage therapist massaged the client's belly, it brought back memories of her mother struggling through her pregnancy alone, and of the client's experience with sexual abuse in college.

When addressing past abuse through cognitive exercises, there may still be residual energy in the chakras. Clearing and rebalancing these chakras can help harmonize the physical, emotional, and energetic bodies. For instance, after a lengthy plane journey, breathing the same air as others and hearing negative conversations, you might feel the need to energetically cleanse yourself. Similarly, if you've faced a health issue linked to a specific chakra, or even if it's been resolved, you might want to direct some loving care to that region. Think of chakra clearing and rebalancing as a way to refresh your soul and energy, similar to how you feel rejuvenated after a good cry. Just as tears can help release old energy and blockages, this process can pave the way for positive new experiences in your life.

7. Vital Vortexes: Activating Your Energy Anatomy

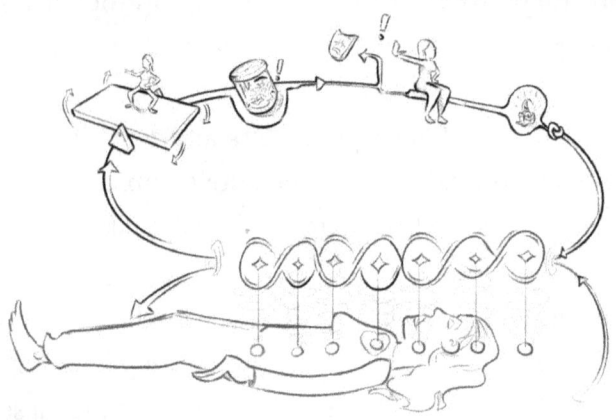

Understanding the Properties of the Beautiful Seven Chakras

Approach each chakra with an open mind and heart and see if you can find any correlations or emotional and behavioral patterns that relate to the chakras. Each chakra has its own emotional, psychological, spiritual, and physical issues that arise when there are imbalances. As the first part of this exercise, write down any of these aspects that you identify with. We will use this information to clear and move the energy in the chakra balancing and energizing exercises.

1. Root Chakra (Muladhara)

Location: Base of the spine

Color: Red

The base chakra serves as a sacred anchor, intimately connecting us to our primal instincts and the earth itself. This fundamental anchor of our existence is deeply rooted in the primal instincts of survival, stability, and security. It is the foundation upon which we build our lives and navigate our earthly experiences.

Individuals with a well-balanced base chakra typically exhibit grounded, practical, and reliable traits. They possess a robust connection to the earth and an innate understanding of the significance of stability in their lives. In the profound style of Caroline Myss, maintaining harmony in the base chakra is essential for fostering a sense of grounding and connectedness in one's life journey.

Psychological imbalances include:

- Low self-esteem and self-worth
- Insecurity and lack of confidence
- Difficulty setting and achieving goals
- Persistent worry about basic needs, such as money, food, and shelter
- Rigid thinking and resistance to change

Emotional imbalances include:

- Anxiety and fear, especially around security and survival
- Anger and frustration
- Feeling ungrounded or unstable
- Difficulty trusting others or oneself
- A sense of not belonging or feeling disconnected from family and community

Spiritual Emotional imbalances include:

- Disconnection from one's spiritual foundation and sense of grounding
- Difficulty in cultivating a strong sense of inner strength and resilience
- Struggles with embracing life's challenges as opportunities for growth
- Lack of gratitude and appreciation for the material world and physical existence

7. Vital Vortexes: Activating Your Energy Anatomy

- Inability to feel connected to the earth and the natural world

Physical imbalances include:

- Issues related to the legs, feet, and lower body
- Lower back pain and sciatica
- Digestive problems and constipation
- Adrenal fatigue and chronic exhaustion
- Weakened immune system

To nourish and maintain a balanced base chakra, one might focus on cultivating behaviors that promote financial stability, prioritize physical health, and establish a safe and secure environment. This includes attending to one's basic needs, creating a stable support system, and recognizing the importance of self-care and personal boundaries.

2. Sacral Chakra (Svadhisthana)

Location: Below the navel
Color: Orange

In the sacral chakra, the realm of creativity, pleasure, and sexuality flourishes, representing our ability to experience joy, passion, and our innate creative power, ultimately fueling the essence of our human journey. A balanced sacral chakra allows for the free-flowing expression of our emotions and facilitates deep connections with others on an emotional level.

Individuals with a harmonious sacral chakra typically embody sensual, creative, and emotionally expressive traits. They embrace the beauty of life, unafraid to delve into the depths of their emotional and creative reservoirs. Cultivating balance within the sacral chakra is essential for tapping into the richness of our emotional and creative landscape.

Psychological imbalances include:
- Low self-esteem and self-worth
- Creativity blocks
- Fear of change or new experiences
- Inability to set and maintain healthy boundaries in relationships
- Difficulty in connecting with one's own desires and needs

Emotional imbalances include:
- Difficulty expressing emotions
- Emotional instability
- Suppressed feelings
- Codependency in relationships
- Lack of passion and zest for life

Spiritual imbalances include:
- Disconnection from one's inner self and intuition
- Struggle with finding life's purpose and meaning
- Difficulty in embracing and expressing one's true nature
- Imbalance in feminine and masculine energies
- Apathy towards spiritual growth and practices

Physical imbalances include:
- Reproductive health issues
- Lower back pain
- Kidney and urinary problems
- Pelvic and hip discomfort
- Digestive system issues

To nurture and balance the sacral chakra, one might engage in artistic pursuits, such as painting, writing, or dancing, in order to channel their creative energy. Additionally, prioritizing pleasure and sensuality, whether through self-care or intimate connections, can help maintain the flow of this vital life force. Fostering healthy relationships, both with oneself and others, is essential in ensuring the emotional well-being associated with this chakra.

3. Solar Plexus Chakra (Manipura)

Location: Above the navel
Color: Yellow

The energy center located above the navel, the solar plexus chakra, serves as a locus for cultivating personal power, self-esteem, and confidence. It empowers us to harness the emotional energy necessary to pursue our goals and dreams and overcome obstacles that may arise on our path. Through the activation and balance of this chakra, we gain the inner strength and self-assurance needed to navigate life's complexities.

Individuals with a balanced solar plexus chakra often embody assertive, decisive, and driven traits. They possess a strong sense of self and are unafraid to assert their boundaries, express their needs, and step into their authentic selves, embracing the full potential of their personal power. Nurturing balance within the solar plexus chakra is crucial for unlocking our inner resilience and drive.

Psychological imbalances include:

- Fear of rejection or failure
- Inability to set and maintain healthy boundaries
- Procrastination and lack of motivation
- Perfectionism and over-analyzing situations
- Dependence on external validation for self-worth

Emotional imbalances include:

- Low self-esteem and lack of self-confidence
- Excessive need for control or power over others
- Difficulty making decisions or trusting one's instincts
- Feeling overwhelmed by responsibility
- Anger, aggression, or passive-aggressiveness

Spiritual imbalances include:

- Disconnection from one's personal power and sense of purpose
- Difficulty in asserting oneself and standing up for one's beliefs
- Imbalance between giving and receiving, leading to burnout or resentment
- Struggles with self-acceptance and embracing one's authentic self
- Difficulty in cultivating a strong sense of inner guidance and intuition

Physical imbalances include:

- Digestive issues, such as ulcers, indigestion, or irritable bowel syndrome (IBS)
- Problems with the liver, gallbladder, pancreas, and stomach
- Chronic fatigue or low energy levels
- Weight gain or issues with metabolism
- Muscle tension, particularly in the abdomen and mid-back

To nurture and maintain harmony within the solar plexus chakra, one might focus on setting clear goals, taking charge of their own life, and developing leadership skills. By fostering self-discipline, resilience, and a strong sense of purpose, they can effectively channel their personal power and confidently forge their own path.

4. Heart Chakra (Anahata)

Location: Center of the chest

Color: Green

At the core of our emotional and spiritual essence resides the heart chakra, nestled within the chest. The heart chakra serves as a conduit to our emotional and spiritual core, guiding the flow of love, compassion, and empathy. This energetic whirlpool allows us to forge profound connections with ourselves and others while opening our hearts to the transformative influence of love.

The heart chakra acts as a fountainhead of joy, gratitude, and forgiveness. Through the activation and harmonization of this chakra, we are empowered to heal emotional scars, release past resentments, and foster a sense of inner serenity and satisfaction.

Those graced with a balanced heart chakra are often distinguished by their loving, empathetic, and nurturing disposition. They remain highly receptive to the emotions of others and are eager to provide their support and comprehension.

Psychological imbalances include:

- Lack of empathy and compassion for self and others
- Difficulty in forming deep, meaningful relationships
- Codependency or unhealthy attachment patterns
- Overly critical or judgmental attitude towards self and others
- Struggling with forgiveness and letting go of past hurts

Emotional imbalances include:

- Difficulty giving or receiving love
- Fear of intimacy and vulnerability
- Feeling unworthy or undeserving of love
- Holding onto past hurts and grudges

- Emotional instability, including mood swings and excessive jealousy

Spiritual imbalances include:
- Disconnection from the feelings of love, unity, and compassion
- Difficulty in experiencing inner peace and harmony
- Struggles with self-love and self-acceptance
- Inability to connect with others on a deeper, spiritual level
- Resistance to opening one's heart to the world and embracing life's challenges with love and compassion

Physical imbalances include:
- Heart-related problems, such as high blood pressure, heart disease, or chest pain
- Respiratory issues, including asthma and bronchitis
- Poor circulation and cold extremities
- Tension and pain in the upper back and shoulders
- Weakened immune system and susceptibility to illness

To nourish and maintain harmony within the heart chakra, one might focus on building deep connections with others, offering emotional support, and practicing acts of kindness. By cultivating a compassionate heart, we can promote healing and growth for ourselves and those around us.

5. Throat Chakra (Vishuddha)
Location: Throat
Color: Blue

The throat chakra serves as a channel for communicating our deepest thoughts, emotions, and truths. Honesty, authenticity, and emotional expression are the defining qualities of a well-balanced throat chakra. When this energetic hub is in harmony, we can share

7. Vital Vortexes: Activating Your Energy Anatomy

our feelings openly and genuinely, nurturing deeper connections and promoting emotional well-being.

Individuals blessed with a balanced throat chakra are frequently distinguished by their eloquent, expressive, and diplomatic dispositions. They possess the skill to articulate their thoughts and emotions effectively, and gracefully maneuver through challenging dialogues with empathy and comprehension.

Psychological imbalances include:

- Low self-esteem or lack of confidence in one's voice
- Communication difficulties or misunderstandings with others
- Social anxiety or fear of public speaking
- Dominating or controlling conversations, or conversely, being excessively passive in communication
- Difficulty in setting and maintaining healthy boundaries with others

Emotional imbalances include:

- Difficulty expressing oneself or speaking one's truth
- Fear of rejection or judgment for expressing opinions
- Inability to listen effectively or empathetically to others
- Suppressed emotions, leading to feelings of frustration or resentment
- Struggles with honesty and authenticity in relationships

Spiritual imbalances include:

- Disconnection from one's inner voice and intuition
- Inability to express and live in alignment with one's true purpose
- Struggles with spiritual or creative expression
- Difficulty in understanding and articulating one's beliefs and values

- Resistance to change and personal growth

Physical imbalances include:

- Throat-related problems, such as sore throat, laryngitis, or thyroid imbalances
- Oral health issues, including toothaches or gum disease
- Neck pain, stiffness, or tension
- Hearing issues or ear infections
- Jaw tension, TMJ disorders, or teeth grinding

To maintain equilibrium within the throat chakra, one might focus on speaking up, sharing ideas, and engaging in open and honest communication. This may involve expressing oneself creatively through writing, art, or music, or engaging in meaningful discussions with friends, family, or colleagues.

6. Third Eye Chakra (Ajna)

Location: Forehead, between the eyebrows
Color: Indigo

The third eye chakra, situated between the eyebrows, acts as a portal to our intuition, insight, and wisdom. This potent energy center enables us to tap into our inherent understanding of the world and access the profound knowledge residing within our consciousness.

Clarity, imagination, and inner vision constitute the emotional aspects of a well-balanced third eye chakra. When this energy hub is in harmony, we can perceive both our inner and outer worlds with lucidity and discernment, allowing our imaginations to flourish and our inner vision to guide us.

Individuals graced with a balanced third eye chakra are frequently distinguished by their intuitive, insightful, and open-minded dispositions. They possess the skill to perceive beyond the surface,

7. Vital Vortexes: Activating Your Energy Anatomy

attuned to the subtle energies and deeper truths hidden beneath the realm of the ordinary.

Psychological imbalances include:

- Lack of clarity and direction in life
- Difficulty making decisions or trusting one's judgment
- Struggles with visualization, memory, or learning
- Over-analyzing situations or becoming stuck in negative thought patterns
- Disconnection from reality, leading to escapism or excessive daydreaming

Emotional imbalances include:

- Difficulty trusting one's intuition or inner guidance
- Fear of the unknown or uncertainty
- Overactive imagination, leading to anxiety or paranoia
- Inability to focus and concentrate
- Emotional instability and mood swings

Spiritual imbalances include:

- Difficulty connecting with one's higher self or spiritual guides
- Inability to perceive or understand the interconnectedness of all things
- Struggles with spiritual growth and awakening
- Closed-mindedness or resistance to new ideas and perspectives
- Difficulty embracing one's innate psychic or intuitive abilities

Physical imbalances include:

- Headaches, migraines, or sinus issues
- Vision problems or eye strain
- Insomnia or sleep disturbances

- Hormonal imbalances or issues with the endocrine system
- Brain fog or cognitive difficulties

To maintain equilibrium within the third eye chakra, one might focus on trusting one's intuition, engaging in meditation, and seeking personal growth and spiritual development. This may involve practices such as mindfulness, journaling, or exploring different spiritual traditions in the pursuit of self-discovery and inner wisdom.

7. Crown Chakra (Sahasrara)
Location: Top of the head
Color: Violet

Positioned at the top of the head, the crown chakra serves as a channel to enlightenment, spirituality, and connection to the divine. This transcendent energy center functions as a bridge between our individual consciousness and the universal consciousness, fostering our spiritual awakening and growth.

A well-balanced crown chakra nurtures inner peace, bliss, and universal love. When this energy hub is harmonious, we experience a profound sense of serenity and interconnectedness, awakening to the boundless love that pervades the universe and imbuing our lives with purpose and meaning.

Individuals graced with a balanced crown chakra typically exhibit wisdom, compassion, and spiritual connectedness. They possess an inherent understanding of the interconnected nature of existence and display a genuine commitment to the well-being of others and the world around them.

Psychological imbalances include:

- Lack of purpose or direction in life

7. Vital Vortexes: Activating Your Energy Anatomy

- Difficulty with self-awareness and self-reflection
- Inability to surrender control or embrace uncertainty
- Excessive attachment to material possessions or external validation
- Over-intellectualizing or excessive rationalization

Emotional imbalances include:

- Feelings of isolation and disconnection from others
- Difficulty experiencing joy, happiness, or inner peace
- Depression, hopelessness, or despair
- Overwhelming feelings of insignificance or unworthiness
- Inability to let go of past hurts or grievances

Spiritual imbalances include:

- Disconnection from one's spiritual nature or higher self
- Inability to experience unity consciousness or a sense of oneness with all things
- Struggles with faith, trust, or belief in a higher power
- Resistance to spiritual growth or personal transformation
- Spiritual apathy, stagnation, or cynicism

Physical imbalances include:

- Headaches, migraines, or tension in the head and neck area
- Insomnia or sleep disturbances
- Issues with the nervous system or neurological disorders
- Hormonal imbalances or issues with the endocrine system
- Weakened immune system or susceptibility to illness

To cultivate equilibrium within the crown chakra, one might engage in spiritual practices, foster a sense of oneness, and embrace a higher purpose in life. This could involve meditation, prayer, volunteer work, or exploring various spiritual traditions to deepen one's connection to the divine and expand one's understanding of the greater cosmic tapestry.

Chakra Balancing and Energizing Exercise

Hidden beliefs, inauthenticity, holding onto resentment, or the exhaustion from becoming new parents due to a newborn's demands can lead to suppressed emotions, which, as I've mentioned, can become lodged within the body. The Chakra Balancing and Energizing Exercise is designed to clear such stuck energy and realign our energetic anatomy.

To start this exercise, close your eyes and direct your focus to your breathing. Take a deep inhale through your nose, letting your abdomen expand as you fill your lungs fully. Then, exhale slowly through your mouth, letting out the air while allowing your abdomen to draw inwards. Continue this deep abdominal breathing for a few minutes, allowing yourself to relax and become centered.

If you're drawn to a specific chakra that feels blocked, give that area a bit more attention during the balancing. It's essential to remember that all chakras are interconnected, so ensure you address each one, allowing them to work in harmony. Dedicate around fifteen to twenty minutes for this routine to get the best outcome. For a guided version of the Chakra Balancing and Energizing Exercise, visit *raydoktor.com* and join Dr. Ray.

Root chakra:

Focus on the base of your spine, where your root chakra is located. As you inhale, visualize a vibrant red light expanding in this area. As you exhale, envision any blockages or imbalances being released. Continue this deep belly breathing, focusing on the red light for a few breaths.

7. Vital Vortexes: Activating Your Energy Anatomy

Sacral chakra:

Move your attention to your sacral chakra, located just below your navel. Visualize an orange light in this area. Inhale deeply, expanding the orange light, and exhale, releasing any blockages. Continue this deep belly breathing, focusing on the orange light for a few breaths.

Solar plexus chakra:

Shift your focus to your solar plexus chakra, located above your navel. Visualize a yellow light in this area. With each deep belly breath, see the yellow light expanding and any blockages being released. Spend a few breaths concentrating on the yellow light.

Heart chakra:

Bring your attention to your heart chakra, located in the center of your chest. Visualize a green light in this area. As you practice deep belly breathing, imagine the green light growing brighter and releasing any imbalances. Breathe deeply and focus on the green light for a few breaths.

Throat chakra:

Focus on your throat chakra, located at the base of your throat. Visualize a blue light in this area. Inhale deeply, expanding the blue light, and exhale, releasing any blockages. Continue this deep belly breathing, focusing on the blue light for a few breaths.

Third eye chakra:

Move your attention to your third eye chakra, located between your eyebrows. Visualize an indigo light in this area. With each deep belly breath, see the indigo light expanding and any blockages being released. Spend a few breaths concentrating on the indigo light.

Crown chakra:

Finally, focus on your crown chakra, located at the top of your head.

Visualize a violet or white light in this area. As you practice deep belly breathing, imagine the light growing brighter and releasing any imbalances. Breathe deeply and focus on the violet or white light for a few breaths.

After spending time with each chakra and feeling a sense of openness throughout your spine and body, visualize all your energy centers shining brightly and aligning seamlessly along your spine. Continue with a few more deep abdominal breaths, tuning into the harmonious flow of energy throughout your body. Gradually ground yourself by anchoring your awareness back to your breath and immediate surroundings. When you're ready, softly open your eyes and take a few moments to reflect on the chakra meditation journey and any insights or feelings that arose during the session. Instead of diving straight into tasks or conversations that could be stressful, ease yourself back in. Consider taking a leisurely walk, resting beneath a tree, indulging in a short nap, or immersing yourself in calming music to solidify the Chakra Balancing and Energizing Exercise within you. You may find that you feel rejuvenated and more receptive. Your perspective may shift, leading to gentler interpretations of events and interactions. This renewed state can feel as if you've taken a mental vacation, reconnecting you with your innate qualities of love, compassion, optimism, and hope.

8
Ascending Beyond Blame: Claiming Personal Sovereignty

In the world of social media, talk shows, and film, people are often portrayed as victims of their past and circumstances. Talk shows like *The Dr. Phil Show* or *The Oprah Winfrey Show* where guests' struggles are often tied to their upbringing. There's a pervasive blame, a sentiment that with better caregivers, life could've been different. Many of us adopt such beliefs about our own relationships and life challenges without questioning them. These views often stem from what we've consistently seen, heard in conversations, and read online.

Often, these portrayals depict individuals who feel unseen, crave positive attention from a parent, or struggle in romantic relationships. Take *Bridget Jones's Diary* as an example. The protagonist, Bridget Jones, embodies the hopeless romantic archetype: lacking confidence, overwhelmed by emotions, and turning to a tub of ice cream after a breakup. Such narratives often depict characters stuck in repetitive patterns, unable to progress psychologically or accept personal responsibility for their unhealthy choices and relationships. Unfortunately, entertainment and gossip that revel in poor conflict resolution skills in relationships shape narratives for both children and adults about what's essential for a happy, fulfilling life.

Rather than portraying empowered individuals on talk shows, in movies, or television series who take personal responsibility—like

8. Ascending Beyond Blame: Claiming Personal Sovereignty

hiring a coach, hitting the gym, journaling, hiking, meditating, or seeking spiritual guidance—modern media often highlights dramatic reactions. After facing setbacks like job loss, betrayal, health scares, or family tragedies, many on-screen characters turn to drinking, impulsive decisions, or self-pity. This focus on drama reflects a society drawn to conflict, possibly because many haven't addressed their own issues.

In traditional therapy, psychologists often discuss issues such as trust, abandonment, or codependent relationship patterns in media outlets. They suggest that these issues originate from one's upbringing or past experiences. Meanwhile, in pop psychology, writers from magazines like *Cosmopolitan, Psychology Today, Men's Health,* and *Glamour* often perpetuate the idea that we are defined by our past and are destined to face life's challenges based on "what happened to us." While our upbringing undoubtedly influences us, we also shape our beliefs and emotions through our interpretations, possibly clinging to these beliefs without questioning their validity or their advantage to us.

It's crucial to assess whether our beliefs truly benefit us. We should consider positive reframing and learn from our past to enhance our lives and relationships beyond what we encountered in childhood. Some hold onto the hope that everything will change with an apology, a return from an ex-partner, hearing "I love you" from a parent, meeting a soulmate, finally achieving financial freedom, or a co-parent fulfilling their obligations. And then, there are those who remain consumed by past accusations, the wrongs they believe they did, constantly seeking validation from others, all the while life continues to blossom and move forward.

It's crucial to remember that while our life experiences may have shaped our personalities, communication style, and how we operate in intimate relationships, it doesn't mean our insecurities are unchangeable, nor should they dictate our future. As mentioned

8. Ascending Beyond Blame: Claiming Personal Sovereignty

throughout this book, we all have hidden beliefs that have secondary gains and unconscious benefits that we might unconsciously perpetuate without knowing it. By doing the emotional and psychological work, we can uncover any belief that's holding us down, surrender the belief altogether, or reach for a higher perspective and understanding that completely shifts our consciousness completely therefore we're no longer the person or consciousness that gets bothered.

For instance, even after establishing a successful coaching business and earning my doctorate in psychology, I anticipated a change in how my parents interacted with me. We had a good relationship, but their communication implied they perceived me as still finding my way. I yearned for their acknowledgment and felt undervalued despite accolades from peers, clients, and social media. It was only after a release ceremony, where I let go of my expectations and the need for their validation, that I experienced genuine lightness around them. Despite my accomplishments, they detected my unhappiness, and as intuitive parents, they were concerned. They recognized my persistent need to prove myself and desired only my inner peace. When I relinquished my ego and abandoned my preconceptions of how they should convey their love to me, I was able to genuinely appreciate them, and they, in turn, embraced the authentic me.

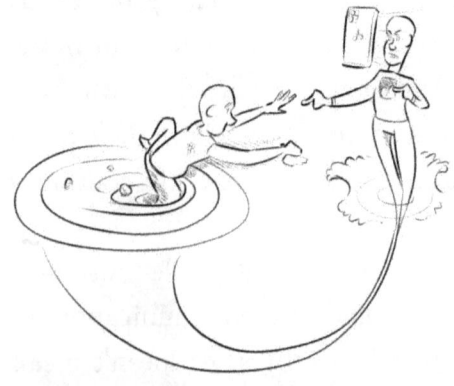

Collective Release Ceremony

Throughout your life, you might have shaped your identity based on waiting for people and circumstances to change. Letting go of these attachments is challenging because they've become familiar markers of our existence. The natural question then arises: "If I no longer identify with my past grievances, if I can't assign blame elsewhere, and if I've long hidden my authentic self in pursuit of acceptance, then who am I in this newfound truth?" Once these barriers are removed, you will become unstoppable, limitless, and free from the invisible anchors that previously held you back.

The Collective Release Ceremony is designed to liberate you from deep-seated hidden beliefs and unquestioned collective narratives. These internalized stories influence your perception of self and your reasons for feeling discontent. Whether they're beliefs you've unknowingly absorbed that shape your life's narratives or habits like laying blame and remaining a victim, these patterns can make it seem like lasting happiness is out of reach or that life consistently deals you a bad hand. This exercise seeks to disrupt that restrictive mindset that limits your viewpoint, encouraging you to see challenges as learning opportunities and to confidently steer your life and relationships in a positive direction.

To maximize the impact of the Collective Release Ceremony, ask for the support of a friend, partner, or coach with whom you can establish trust and share your vulnerabilities. Have them read each statement, making sure they provide enough time for you to fully engage in the experience and relinquish any remaining attachments. Set aside at least thirty minutes for this exercise. Alternatively, you can record yourself reading each statement on your phone or another device, remembering to insert pauses between each sentence stem. To experience the Collective Release Ceremony guided by Dr. Ray, visit *raydoktor.com/tools*.

8. Ascending Beyond Blame: Claiming Personal Sovereignty

Choose a comfortable location where you won't be disturbed for your release ceremony, ensuring that you'll feel at ease if you cry or make loud noises. Playing meditative music without vocals or lyrics can help enhance the experience. During the process, you may experience catharsis and various physical sensations as you release both personal and collective energies. You might feel shaking or an electric-like energy coursing through your body.

Emotional responses can range from sadness to sudden bursts of laughter. Allow yourself to perceive colors, images, or whatever your imagination offers as a means to release what you need to let go of. You may notice changes in body temperature and breathing patterns. Take care of yourself, stay hydrated, and give yourself permission to stop if the experience becomes too challenging.

Feel free to disregard the sentences that don't seem to apply to you. However, remember that these are energies our collective consciousness needs to release, just as if you were a Tibetan monk praying for peace for all.

Collective Release Ceremony Sentences

I take responsibility for my creation of the archetypal **father** within my mind. I release any tension in my body and energy field that arises from expectations and attachments to his words, actions, and the version of him I long for, extending to the outer limits of his energy and existence. I allow compassion to transform our relationship for the greater good of all.

I take responsibility for my creation of the archetypal **mother** within my mind. I release any tension in my body and energy field that arises from expectations and attachments to her words, actions, and the version of her I long for, extending to the outer limits of her energy and existence. I allow compassion to transform our relationship for the greater good of all.

I take responsibility for my creation of the archetypal **grandparents** within my mind. I release any tension in my body and energy field that arises from expectations and attachments to their words, actions, and the version of them I long for, extending to the outer limits of their energy and existence. I allow compassion to transform our relationship for the greater good of all.

I take responsibility for creating the belief that I'm not a **good parent** and should feel bad for not doing better. I release any tension in my body and energy field associated with feeling like I'm not a good parent and the guilt for not doing better, extending to the outer limits of its influence and existence. I invite compassion to transform my relationship with my parenting for the greater good of all.

I take responsibility for creating the belief in my mind that I **need to become a parent** to experience a better life. I release any tension in my body and energy field that arises from expectations and attachments to the need to become a parent, extending to the outer limits of its influence and existence. I allow compassion to transform my need to become a parent for the greater good of all.

I take responsibility for creating the concept of the **perfect co-parent** within my mind. I release any tension in my body and energy field that arises from expectations and attachments to the perfect co-parent, extending to the outer limits of its influence and existence. I allow compassion to transform my relationship with my co-parent for the greater good of all.

8. Ascending Beyond Blame: Claiming Personal Sovereignty

I take responsibility for my creation of the concept of **success** within my mind. I release any tension in my body and energy field that arises from expectations and attachments to success, reaching the outer limits of its influence and existence. I allow compassion to transform my relationship with success for the greater good of all.

I take responsibility for creating the concept of **perfection** within my mind. I release any tension in my body and energy field that arises from expectations and attachments to perfectionism, extending to the outer limits of its influence and existence. I allow compassion to transform my relationship with perfectionism for the greater good of all.

I take responsibility for creating the concept of **physical appearance** within my mind. I release any tension in my body and energy field that arises from expectations and attachments to physical appearance, reaching the outer limits of its influence and existence. I allow compassion to transform my relationship with physical appearance for the greater good of all.

I take responsibility for creating the belief of **needing an apology** within my mind to move forward in my life. I release any tension in my body and energy field that arises from expectations and attachments to needing an apology, reaching the outer limits of its influence and existence. I allow compassion to transform my relationship with the need for an apology for the greater good of all.

I take responsibility for creating any negativity surrounding my calendar **age** within my mind. I release any tension in my body and energy field that arises from expectations and attachments to my calendar age, extending to the outer limits of its influence and existence. I allow compassion to transform my relationship with my calendar age for the greater good of all.

I take responsibility for creating the belief in my mind that I need to be in an **intimate relationship** to experience a better life. I release any tension in my body and energy field that arises from expectations and attachments to the need for an intimate relationship, reaching the outer limits of its influence and existence. I allow compassion to cultivate the healthiest and most loving relationship with myself for the greater good of all.

I take responsibility for creating the belief in my mind that I need **respect** to feel worthy. I release any tension in my body and energy field that arises from expectations and attachments to needing respect from others, reaching the outer limits of its influence and existence. I allow compassion to transform my relationship with respect for the greater good of all.

I take responsibility for creating the concept of **guilt** for doing something wrong within my mind. I release any tension in my body and energy field that arises from expectations and attachments to guilt for doing something wrong, reaching the outer limits of its influence and existence. I allow compassion to transform my relationship with guilt for the greater good of all.

I take responsibility for creating the belief in my mind that **I'm supposed to be liked** and get along with everyone. I release any tension in my body and energy field that arises from expectations and attachments to the belief that I need to be liked, extending to the outer limits of its influence and existence. I allow compassion to transform

8. Ascending Beyond Blame: Claiming Personal Sovereignty

my relationship with the need to be liked for the greater good of all.

I take responsibility for creating the belief that **I'm not enough** within my mind. I release any tension in my body and energy field that arises from expectations and attachments to the belief that I'm not enough, extending to the outer limits of its influence and existence. I allow compassion to transform my relationship with the belief that I'm not enough for the greater good of all.

I take responsibility for creating the belief in my mind that **I'm supposed to be somewhere** else in my life. I release any tension in my body and energy field that arises from expectations and attachments to the belief that I'm supposed to be somewhere else, reaching the outer limits of its influence and existence. I allow compassion to transform my relationship with the belief that I'm supposed to be somewhere else for the greater good of all.

I take responsibility for creating the concept in my mind that I have **bad karma** for doing something wrong. I release any tension in my body and energy field that arises from expectations and attachments to the concept of having bad karma, extending to the outer limits of its influence and existence. I allow compassion to transform my belief about karma, fostering the most loving relationship with myself for the greater good of all.

I take responsibility for creating the belief that I have too much or not enough **masculinity or femininity** within my mind. I release any tension in my body and energy field that arises from not feeling balanced with my masculine or feminine aspects, extending to the outer limits of their influence and existence. I allow compassion to transform my relationship with my masculinity and femininity for the greater good of all.

I take responsibility for creating the belief in my mind that **I'm supposed to get along with my family.** I release any tension in my body and energy field that arises from expectations and attachments to the belief that I'm supposed to get along with my family, reaching the outer limits of its influence and existence. I allow compassion to transform my relationship with the belief that I'm supposed to get along with my family for the greater good of all.

I take responsibility for creating the belief in my mind that my **efforts and accomplishments** need to be validated by others. I release any tension in my body and energy field that arises from expectations and attachments to the belief that my efforts and accomplishments need to be validated by others, extending to the outer limits of its influence and existence. I allow compassion to transform my relationship with the belief that my efforts and accomplishments need to be validated by others for the greater good of all.

I take responsibility for creating the belief in my mind that my life is what it is today because of the **past**. I release any tension in my body and energy field that arises from expectations and attachments to the belief that my life is what it is today because of the past, reaching the outer limits of its influence and existence. I allow compassion to transform my relationship with the past for the greater good of all.

I take responsibility for creating the belief in my mind that my **life was supposed to work** out a different way. I release any tension in my body and energy field that arises from expectations and attachments

8. Ascending Beyond Blame: Claiming Personal Sovereignty

to the belief that my life was supposed to be different from what it is today, reaching the outer limits of its influence and existence. I allow compassion to transform my relationship with myself and accept where I am with love for the greater good of all.

I take responsibility for creating the belief in my mind that my happiness and the expansion of my life are **limited by my physical state**. I release any tension in my body and energy field arising from expectations and attachments to the belief that my body should be different from what it is today, extending to the outer limits of its influence and existence. I allow compassion to transform my relationship with my body image and expectations of how my body should function for the greater good of all.

I take responsibility for creating the belief that my life is what it is because **I'm different**. I release any tension in my body and energy field that arises from expectations and attachments to the belief that my life is what it is today because I'm different, extending to the outer limits of its influence and existence. I allow compassion to transform my relationship with the belief that I'm different for the greater good of all.

I take responsibility for creating the belief that I don't **trust** myself and that others need to earn my trust for me to feel safe. I release any tension in my body and energy field that arises from expectations and attachments to not trusting myself, extending to the outer limits of its influence and existence. I allow compassion to transform my relationship with trust for the greater good of all.

I take responsibility for creating the concept of **confidence** and the belief that it's something I need to become, rather than being born confident. I release any tension in my body and energy field that arises

8. Ascending Beyond Blame: Claiming Personal Sovereignty

from expectations and attachments to the belief that I lack confidence, extending to the outer limits of its influence and existence. I allow compassion to transform my relationship with confidence for the greater good of all.

Beloved Divine Presence, as I conclude this sacred invocation, I stand in gratitude and reverence for the transformative power of Your infinite love and wisdom. I acknowledge the divine light that shines within me, guiding me towards greater understanding, healing, and growth.

In the sacred space of my heart, I release all that no longer serves my highest good, making room for the blessings and grace of Your eternal love to flow into my life. As I embrace the beauty of my divine nature, I become a beacon of light for others, embodying the peace, love, and harmony that radiate from Your essence.

May my heart be filled with gratitude, my mind with clarity, and my spirit with the unwavering certainty of Your guidance, as I continue on my journey towards wholeness and unity with the Divine. In the infinite abundance of Your love, I am forever supported, nourished, and uplifted.

And so it is, with deep gratitude, that I affirm and accept the truth of my divine connection, knowing that all is unfolding according to Your divine plan. In Your holy name, I release my words into the Universal Law, trusting in the perfect expression of my intentions.

As it is said, so it is.
Amen.

This exercise is typically performed only once. However, if you encounter an obstacle or find it challenging to let go of a specific collective or personal belief, you might revisit it. It can be beneficial

8. Ascending Beyond Blame: Claiming Personal Sovereignty

to return to the exercise periodically, as our consciousness is always expanding, and we may have a different experience and new insights. It's similar to rereading an old book and discovering value we hadn't recognized during a previous read.

If you feel called to create your own sentences to release beliefs that no longer serve you, simply fill in the blank with what you want to release, adjusting the sentence to fit your needs:

> I take responsibility for my creation of _____ within my mind. I release any tension in my body and energy field that arises from expectations and attachments to _____, extending to the outer limits of its energy and existence. I allow compassion to transform _____ for the greater good of all.

As you grow and align more with your true self, your perspectives on life, relationships, and yourself will naturally shift. It's often said that the journey matters more than the destination, and this sentiment is especially true for healing. Embrace your evolving self. With patience and dedication to these transformative processes, you'll find that life, love, and relationships become richer, ushering in a rejuvenated you.

9
The Shadow Dance: Navigating Personality Friction

In moments of stress or when overwhelmed by collective narratives of negativity, fears such as not being able to pay bills can resurface. If we haven't addressed our past childhood wounds or taken time for self-reflection, we might remain unaware of when we've behaved inappropriately. And if someone tries to point it out, our defensiveness might push them away. Such states can lead us to imagine the worst, dominate conversations without genuinely listening, constantly complain, or slip into a victim mentality. These behaviors can result in Personality Friction Points, where we either inadvertently push people away or find ourselves isolated because others prefer to steer clear of us.

Interestingly, these Personality Friction Points often align with the shadow aspects and communication patterns of the archetypal characters we embody. For instance, in Caregiver mode, we might over-apologize or lean into people-pleasing, whereas the Ruler archetype may lead us to dominate conversations and display excessive control. We might also manifest a pessimistic Rebel attitude, resulting in frequent complaints, and coming across as a downer to others. Reflecting on the shadows of the archetypes we embody can offer valuable insight into how others might perceive us during our challenging moments.

9. The Shadow Dance: Navigating Personality Friction

We all have challenging days, particularly when faced with multiple stressors and interactions. My shadow behaviors, linked to the Personality Friction Points of the Know-It-All and the Commander, may manifest as impatience, a controlling nature, a lack of openness to others' perspectives—especially regarding psychology and the healing arts—or an appearance of being closed off, stemming from a "been there, done that" attitude. This behavior can make me seem closed off or even arrogant. Those close to me are aware of this aspect of my personality. I welcome their feedback and support, especially during stressful times.

A significant issue arises when we, or others, perceive these negative personality traits as our core nature, or when we are so guarded that there is little room for mutual engagement. This hinders the development of reciprocal relationships because our shadow side influences our decisions, emotions, and communication style. By being more forgiving and light-hearted about ourselves, and being transparent with others, we allow our loved ones to understand our challenges. This ensures they don't feel the need to tread lightly and can readily offer support when our stress is evident.

Becoming self-aware is crucial, especially during disagreements. Taking a mental pause and managing our immediate emotions mid-sentence requires mastery. However, it becomes simpler once we address our negative hidden beliefs and understand our archetypal shadows. Recognizing this allows us to soften our approach, prioritize connection, and communicate more gently. It prevents us from letting stress-driven behaviors sabotage conversations, ensuring we don't speak from fear, appear controlling, or try to appease everyone. Instead, we can remain authentic.

Here are ten Personality Friction Points commonly observed in conversations. You might recognize these communication and personality styles in yourself or someone you know, especially during conversations, group meetings, or stressful situations. This isn't about judging ourselves or others but about bringing awareness to communication styles that might be hidden from us and understanding the reasons behind them. Recognizing these patterns can help us reflect on our behaviors, consider changes if desired, and cultivate compassion for those who may be communicating from a place of insecurity or fear.

Ten Personality Friction Points

The Interviewer is a personality friction point that focuses on asking questions, keeping the spotlight on the other person. While this may aim to make the other person feel good, it often results in a one-sided conversation where the Interviewer doesn't let others get to know him. It can be a method to dodge vulnerability and deflect during conversations. Many people enjoy being the center of attention and may talk endlessly. However, the Interviewer may not be genuinely interested in the other person. In extreme cases, this behavior can turn negative, potentially serving as a tactic to gather information for manipulation or personal gain.

9. The Shadow Dance: Navigating Personality Friction

The Complainer is a personality friction point that often defines itself as a victim of life conspiring against them. They frequently seek sympathetic ears for their grievances and tend to focus on the negative aspects of their lives. Portraying a pessimistic view, they blame the past, situations, and others for their troubles. When with empathetic individuals, attention usually shifts to the Complainer, as others may feel the urge to comfort. The Complainer often avoids personal responsibility, becoming immersed in their persistent negative narrative. As a result, they might twist even positive stories into tales of distress. They often struggle to genuinely celebrate others' successes, steering conversations back to their own hardships. This can lead to passive-aggressive comments, rooted in feelings of envy or resentment.

The Commander is a personality friction point characterized by a strong desire to control and direct others. They often feel most comfortable when in charge, even in situations where it might not be appropriate. They may critique the staff, comment on the ambiance like room temperature or the quality of food and attempt to control their surroundings to feel at ease. This communication style might have developed from being raised by a bossy parent. Beneath the Commander's seemingly guarded and rigid exterior often lies a sense of insecurity and a feeling of being out of control. They may struggle to trust others to contribute, support them, or complete tasks the way they would. Their reluctance to show vulnerability and allow others to truly know them can create barriers to genuine connections in their relationships.

The Advisor is a personality friction point with a tendency to offer opinions and unsolicited advice, regardless of their knowledge on a specific topic. While there may be genuine intentions to help others *fix* issues, they often become more absorbed in their emotions and how they would address situations, rather than truly listening and connecting to others' feelings. Even when others are merely sharing without implying a problem to be fixed, the Advisor may not genuinely listen. Instead of adopting a humble stance and being open to learning, they frequently focus on giving advice on any topic that comes up. Unconsciously, the Advisor might act this way to impress someone or to appear more knowledgeable and useful. However, this inclination to *fix* unbroken situations or people can hinder conversation and prevent them from establishing deep, meaningful connections with others.

The Disrupter is a personality friction point who often interrupts others during conversations. They seem more interested in sharing their own views than in allowing others to complete their thoughts. This communication style is usually unintentional; the Disrupter may be reacting to triggers they aren't conscious of or could be in a trauma response, overwhelmed by their own emotions and narrative. This pattern of interruption can serve as a defense mechanism, helping the Disrupter dodge vulnerability, divert from unwanted subjects, or simply remain oblivious to the conversational needs of others. At times, deliberate disruptions can be beneficial, such as lightening a heavy mood or addressing difficult topics humorously, much like a comedian. However, if individuals are repeatedly interrupted, they may withdraw from the conversation. While it's essential for discussions to have purpose, they should also flow naturally without rigid expectations.

The Avoider is a personality friction point characterized by a tendency to deflect questions and resist direct answers. This behavior often stems from an effort to avoid vulnerability, usually due to fear of revealing insecurities or lacking confidence. In extreme situations, when the possibility of becoming the center of attention arises, the Avoider might experience heightened anxiety and nervousness, which can lead them to physically withdraw from the scenario. They

9. The Shadow Dance: Navigating Personality Friction

typically have difficulty establishing true intimacy, both with others and themselves. In social contexts, they may shy away from deep conversations and instead use tactics like posing questions to others, making jokes, or steering the dialogue towards more outspoken individuals to avert genuine connection. While at times, avoiding certain people and discussions can be an exercise in setting healthy boundaries, more often than not, Avoiders are shying away from the deeper self-exploration required to address and heal their insecurities, both consciously and unconsciously.

The Know-It-All is a personality friction point characterized by an unyielding conviction in their own knowledge. Believing they are more intelligent than others, Know-It-Alls are convinced of their superior insights and methods for tackling situations. They tend to be closed to new ideas and lack genuine curiosity, often giving the impression that they have everything figured out. In conversations, they may interject with phrases such as "I know," "I've done that before," or "I've been there before," even while others are speaking. They may appear uninterested when others share, persistently steering the conversation back to their own perspectives and beliefs, convinced of their complete accuracy. Engaging with a Know-It-All can be difficult, as they are not open to relating or collaborating, often expecting others to simply accept their supposed wisdom and insights, which diminishes the opportunity for genuine connection and shared understanding.

The Class Clown is a personality friction point characterized by constant humor and avoidance of serious conversation. Known for making jokes in nearly any situation, including inappropriate moments, this individual often participates in conversations involving deep intimacy or vulnerability, using humor to break the ice or deflect attention from themselves. They may find it challenging to engage in serious discussions or handle emotionally charged matters. While

9. The Shadow Dance: Navigating Personality Friction

the Class Clown's presence is often enjoyed for bringing laughter and lighter energy to social gatherings, their comical nature can become disrespectful or tiresome when it lacks substance. Behind the jovial exterior, the Class Clown may conceal inner sadness or loneliness, using humor to ensure they are liked and to create a lighter atmosphere rather than confronting difficult times and challenges. Life is not always a party, and potential intimate partners may feel they cannot reach a deeper connection or be taken seriously by the Class Clown.

The Challenger is a personality friction point that constantly challenges everything they hear. They are opinionated, often resembling a rebel without a cause. According to them, their views on politics or societal norms are always the correct ones. Typically, people can tolerate them only in small doses, as they seem to create conflict for no apparent reason. They consistently sound oppositional, even when they are in agreement. The Challenger might describe themselves as simply skeptical or assert that they are not sheep, attributing their demeanor to trust issues. However, others often perceive them as being constantly pessimistic. There is a possibility that they grew up in an environment filled with constant debates and a lack of harmony, which may have unconsciously shaped their communication style. Their interactions can always feel more like a challenge or competition than a connective conversation.

The Dominator is a personality friction point who dominates every conversation, drawing all the attention to themselves. They do most of the talking, often turning the dialogue into a monologue. While they might be an interesting individual, cultured and knowledgeable about life and history, they still end up dominating the conversations. Many people are trapped in their insecurities and do not want to tell someone to stop talking. As a result, they simply act politely and smile while the Dominator continues to speak. Desiring to be liked,

9. The Shadow Dance: Navigating Personality Friction

the Dominator might believe that their vast knowledge and ability to discuss various topics make them more attractive. However, they may not know how to read the room and recognize that others have not had much opportunity to contribute to the conversation, leaving them feeling unheard and uncared for. The Dominator often falls short in creating reciprocal connections, never truly getting to know anyone at parties, business meetings, or lunches.

Cultivating a Spiritual Partnership and Deeper Connections through Authentic, Loving Feedback

Many of us fall into one or more of these personality friction points when we are stressed. If more of us took feedback less personally and refrained from becoming defensive, we would have fewer rough edges around us, and people would connect with us more easily. This is because we would be more receptive to feedback from people, situations, and life itself, applying it in a healthy, constructive manner to soften our rigid personalities.

Our closest friends usually recognize when we are in a dark place, dealing with multiple stressors, whether related to finances, relationships, or an expensive home repair. We might come across as short-tempered, strained, pessimistic, or angry, but those who care about us understand that this might not be a true reflection of our character. They might accept our personalities, avoid us during these times, or tolerate us in small doses when we are under stress.

Regrettably, valuable insights from those closest to us often go unshared due to our defensiveness, their fear of losing the friendship, or because they too have their own inner struggles and wouldn't want anyone to critique their personality or communication skills. This crucial feedback, which we need to hear, is frequently reserved for coaching sessions when it's already too late. The transparency in relationships we need often holds the precious nuggets of wisdom essential for saving our marriages, businesses, health, and overall well-being. If we were more open to receiving these insights from those who care about us, many of our friendships, business partnerships, and other relationships might have avoided ending.

Healthy conflict resolution is crucial for maintaining sustainable and nourishing relationships. Everything may appear ideal during the honeymoon phase or at the start of a thrilling new venture, such as a startup. However, significant life transitions—be it death, divorce, relocation, job loss, health challenges, or emerging unhealed traumas—inevitably impact all relationships. Despite attempts to compartmentalize or uphold professionalism, no one is immune to life's stressors, which often expose personality friction points in communication when we're under tremendous stress. Recognizing how stress impacts us and those with whom we spend the most time is key to fostering healthy, problem-solving communication. It enables us to reach agreements even under stress, forgive misunderstandings, offer simple apologies, and progress in a renewed, positive, and growth-oriented manner.

When I first delved into the world of healing and coaching, working alongside esteemed healers, authors, and health practitioners, I often encountered surprisingly poor communication styles and unprofessional behavior. Despite their deep expertise, some exhibited disappointing bedside manners. Their brilliance in their respective crafts seemed to shield them from criticism. If confronted, they would become defensive and condescending, shying away from taking personal responsibility. Constructive feedback was often swiftly redirected, implying the issue lay with the student or client. The assumption that the teacher or healer knows best often overshadowed any input from those seeking guidance. Proficiency in their field didn't exempt them from poor communication; they sometimes behaved insensitively, just like anyone else. Accomplished individuals are human too and

9. The Shadow Dance: Navigating Personality Friction

may have adopted their unhealthy hidden communication styles from traumatic childhood experiences, cultural influences, or parents who modeled poor communication. They may excel in their fields, yet still struggle with communication when stressed.

Often, we fail to address our rigid personalities and communication styles when we're under a lot of stress and wholly absorbed in resolving our problems, such as addiction, divorce, health challenges, working on trust issues, or trying to find the source of our anger. We neglect to consider how we talk, who we're becoming, how we're behaving, how we're speaking, and how we're treating others. We become so preoccupied with fixing what we perceive as the problem that neither we nor anyone else monitors our personality, behaviors, and communication style.

I pose three questions to potential romantic partners early in the relationship, and I adapt these questions to suit a professional context when considering a collaboration. While the phrasing may vary, my goal remains consistent: to understand how a person communicates and behaves under stress. Gaining insight into someone's stress communication style is crucial for establishing a healthy framework that helps prevent future challenges and potential breakdowns in the relationship.

How do you communicate when you're under a lot of stress or facing challenges?

How do you recognize when you're experiencing stress, or how do I recognize it? For example, do you communicate differently, withdraw, or become impatient? Is there a noticeable change that you're aware of?

If I notice you're under stress, how can I best support you in a way that you'll be receptive to? Is there something specific I could say that works best for you?

Nurturing Stronger Ties: The Feedback and Growth Challenge

I invite you to take the opportunity to understand and heal any *hidden* personality friction points and communication, especially in relationships where you seek to strengthen bonds, create deeper connections, and eliminate awkwardness. This exercise aims to address the "elephant in the room" that everyone avoids discussing, enabling more authenticity, transparency, and understanding.

Identify three to five people who have consistently experienced your communication style and who you believe will be honest with you. They don't necessarily have to be close friends, but people with whom you've interacted frequently and in different contexts. Try to include a mix of genders for varied perspectives.

The following is a suggested way to approach the conversation with the person from whom you're seeking feedback: "I'm undertaking a life coaching exercise aimed at improving my communication skills and overall presence. I'd like to ask you five questions and would genuinely appreciate your honest and transparent observations of me. I promise not to become defensive or hold anything you share with me against you. I won't respond until a day later to allow myself time to absorb and integrate the valuable feedback you've provided. I'll get back to you after I've fully processed your honest feedback."

Ask the following 5 questions:
1. What do you see working well in my life?
2. Where in my life do you see something not working very well? And if you were me, what would you do?
3. What do you feel are my greatest strengths and weaknesses?
4. Have I done anything that has hurt you or that still bothers you?
5. Are there ways that could make you feel more comfortable and trusting with me?

9. The Shadow Dance: Navigating Personality Friction

This feedback exercise tends to yield a high degree of accuracy regarding your behavioral, archetypal, and emotional patterns. If there are any unresolved issues or resentments, this exercise could alleviate and heal any tension between you and the person involved, thereby fostering deeper trust and a stronger bond. The best part is that these people already understand and accept these traits, so they are not passing judgment—they remain your friends and continue to communicate with you. Of course, their responses might include their own projections onto you. Regardless, there is immense value in this process for quickly identifying and addressing hidden aspects of ourselves that may push people away.

You may encounter a range of opinions about yourself from your friends and those with whom you interact regularly, some of which might seem far from your own perceived truth. Understandably, their perspectives are shaped by the context in which they have experienced you, such as if you used to work with them or if they were an ex-romantic partner.

Nevertheless, pay attention to the common threads that emerge from their feedback. Consider these shared observations as potential truths and use them as opportunities for self-improvement. This could mean adjusting a behavior, softening your communication style, relaxing your facial expressions, speaking from the heart, or adopting other suggestions that could make you more authentic, approachable, and enjoyable to be around. Regardless of whether their feedback is entirely accurate, adopting these changes can only contribute to a healthier, improved version of yourself.

10
Illuminated Paths: Steering Through the Continuum of Self-Healing

The tools, life-affirming philosophies, and the reframing of your experiences provided in this book serve as a manual for living the best version of yourself. They aim to guide you in crafting an exceptional life, equipping you to tackle your challenges with greater grace, compassion, confidence, and trust. I do not expect a single reading of this book to unveil all the answers or render you invulnerable to future challenges. Rather, my intention is to help you clear away the substantial obstacles of entrenched emotions and negative beliefs that weigh you down, enabling you to ascend like a phoenix into the sky—unburdened by your past and endowed with ultimate emotional freedom.

Throughout my career, I've observed countless clients and workshop participants transform behaviors and eliminate emotional triggers, never to face them again. However, life will continue to present us with unexpected curveballs for our learning and personal expansion. Some things will be easy to let go of; you can change your behavior with little effort, and some things might be recurring themes in your life that take more time to understand and shift. Nevertheless, by removing hidden beliefs and gaining clarity on how you want to show up in life, regardless of your past, you will navigate new challenges with greater ease, and they won't dominate your headspace with negativity.

10. Illuminated Paths: Steering Through the Continuum of Self-Healing

In my experience, when individuals start their transformational journey and begin to see tangible benefits—increased vitality, more genuine relationships, and less drama in their lives—they often want to continue and delve deeper into the path of self-development. It's easy to become enthralled with the feeling of well-being and to crave learning new life skills.

Sometimes, our curiosity is piqued by a friend recommending a new technique or teacher to try. At other times, we may feel that our current methods or teachings have taken us as far as they can, much like earning a master's degree and then seeking a Ph.D. to further our understanding of consciousness and the art of living happily and healthily.

And, of course, there are times when the issue arises from not properly applying and integrating what we've learned. We might mistakenly believe that our tools are ineffective, or assume that there is something better out there, instead of realizing that we might be hastening our healing process or not fully implementing the lessons we've gathered so far. For me, my negative pattern in approaching the healing arts closely mirrored the way I lived my life before beginning my journey—always in the fast lane, seldom resting or pausing, and not fully internalizing, or as one might say, "smelling the roses" that I had already pruned.

You may still have questions about your healing journey. It's common to encounter challenges while exploring new methods with different practitioners. Discussions about your progress and the next steps might arise among friends. Doubts about your intuition or confusion from mixed messages may surface. Like most, you're likely to encounter the potential *shadows* within the healing arts. Regardless of the church, teacher, or approach that resonates with you, our collective human experience of healing and redefining well-being means we'll face both darkness and light. In this chapter, I offer insights to help you discern truth from falsehood and navigate these potential challenges.

10. Illuminated Paths: Steering Through the Continuum of Self-Healing

What if I don't Like the Practitioner or Modality?

Consider this scenario: You've decided to work with a personal trainer at the gym. You notice improvements in your physical body, but sometimes you might not enjoy the exercises, or your body may become sore after an intense workout. Since you associate soreness with a good workout, you believe the personal trainer is delivering the expected results. Changing your body composition inevitably demands new habits, consistent effort, occasional discomfort, and at times, pushing through self-doubt.

Would experiencing your personal trainer as a friend be important to you? Would you tolerate poor communication, subpar bedside manners, differing values, excessive chatter, or potential personality conflicts if you were seeing positive results from their training? If you are a highly sensitive person prone to taking things personally, you might find yourself constantly irritated. This could render your experience with the personal trainer counterproductive because instead of fully reaping the rewards of the training and enjoying good conversations, you might find yourself continuously upset over the interactions and potential miscommunications.

10. Illuminated Paths: Steering Through the Continuum of Self-Healing

Early in my healing journey, I discovered an intriguing book authored by a doctor in Los Angeles. I reached out and we arranged a meeting at his home office. During our session, he abruptly left to take a phone call from his VIP client—who, I later found out, was his primary source of income. His lack of professionalism was off-putting. It was at odds with my work ethic and highlighted a misalignment between my expectations and his manner of engaging with clients. I chose not to work with him again, and when I communicated this decision, he tried to chastise me by saying I needed to get my priorities straight. At only twenty-two, his words left me confused, but I was confident in my decision that this practitioner was not the right fit for me.

Whoever you choose to work with, the experience should be steeped in transparency—including your concerns and questions. It's a partnership, after all. Certainly, there may be elements they can't fully elucidate—sometimes things work without a clear explanation. Or perhaps a client isn't quite ready, peppering the conversation with endless questions because they're hesitant. Nonetheless, the practitioner you collaborate with should provide the space for you to communicate openly, without fear of judgment, or a reluctance to answer your questions. Boasting about credentials and testimonials, while turning a deaf ear to your needs, is not the hallmark of a tuned-in professional. The relationship with the practitioner could be a chance to flex new muscles—such as practicing radical honesty, asserting boundaries, or advocating for oneself. The dynamic between client and practitioner is profoundly relational, thus it's essential to sense whether there's an alignment with your values.

Practitioners under stress may exhibit shadows of their personality. Nevertheless, as a patient or client, you stand as an equal, fully deserving of respect and certainly not deserving of mistreatment, especially when you are compensating them for their services. If their behavior reflects personal struggles—such as grieving over a recently deceased spouse—it may be indicative of their current incapacity to work effectively due to their emotional state and processing. Their judgment may be impaired, or they might simply be uncentered. As the client, it may fall to you to discern their readiness to practice, even if they continue to see clients.

In the realms of healing, spirituality, and wellness, you might meet individuals who come across as unconventional or awkward. Their introverted nature, sensitivity, or eccentricity should be met with unconditional acceptance, especially if they show care and genuine concern for your wellbeing. Practicing personal responsibility is key—it involves open communication, questioning, setting boundaries, and trusting your intuition. It's important to recognize when it's not just resistance to discomfort that's causing hesitation, but a true misalignment in values, or a crossed boundary, signaling that it's not the right match. This process underscores the value of discernment and listening to both your heart and intuition, irrespective of glowing testimonials. Researching through referrals and reviews, and evaluating your direct experiences with a practitioner, are essential in determining if their approach suits your personal needs.

Navigating the Guru-Client Relationship

Remember not to idealize an unreachable archetype of the *perfect healer*. Healers, like everyone else, have their own history and *hidden beliefs*. The stories of miraculous healers, gurus, and swamis are entrenched in our culture and shape our expectations.

Engaging with a spiritual guide, it's easy to place them on a pedestal, expecting them to be the sole catalyst for our healing. Such projections can stem from our unresolved familial needs and from neglecting personal responsibility. This mindset can foster an unhealthy guru-disciple dynamic, blurring boundaries and leaving our core issues unaddressed.

10. Illuminated Paths: Steering Through the Continuum of Self-Healing

Enthralled by their stories and wisdom, it's essential to assess these figures as individuals and gauge the congruence of their values with ours. We must be proactive in our self-transformation; a genuine teacher reflects our potential and ignites our self-awareness. They offer insights that can promote healing, but it's up to us to apply these lessons.

If something feels off or we don't see the growth we hoped for, trust your judgment, and reassess your choice of teacher. Our interactions with teachers should mirror those we have with potential friends or partners—mutual respect and acknowledgment are key. If this reciprocity falters, it's time to rethink our engagement, regardless of their reputation.

Acknowledging our role in self-improvement is critical. We mustn't hand over our agency to anyone, especially if we're prone to depending on others for solutions or if we're struggling with experiencing our own personal power. Our innate capacity for change is the cornerstone of growth. Teachers are there to offer insights and frameworks; however, the work of healing rests with us.

Your Body, Your Rules: Asserting Boundaries for Personal Wellness

Unless you're receiving a massage or required to expose a part of your body for examination or treatment by a practitioner, there is no reason why you should be undressed or touched without prior discussion and clear consent. It's crucial that these conversations occur ahead of time, ensuring you aren't pressured into a decision until you feel safe and trust the process. If needed, bring a friend or other support person with you, if appropriate.

Remember, it's your prerogative to tell the practitioner to stop at any point if you feel uncomfortable. A well-trained practitioner will engage in transparent discussions, informing you about the procedure

10. Illuminated Paths: Steering Through the Continuum of Self-Healing

and what you can expect. If touch is involved, they should be attentive to your needs and continuously check in with you, asking questions such as, "How are you feeling?" and "Is this okay for you?"

This respectful approach should be followed by anyone providing physical body work or therapeutic manipulation. Regrettably, there have been instances where individuals have been shamed for their hesitation, told that their discomfort is simply *resistance* that must be overcome for healing to occur. While there may be some truth to this, it's essential to remember that in such vulnerable moments, individuals may feel confused or disoriented. Therefore, they should be encouraged to feel more grounded and present before proceeding.

It's important to acknowledge that abuse from a practitioner is never acceptable, nor is simplifying complex situations with "everything happens for a reason," particularly when working through unresolved issues. However, personal experiences and those of many clients have taught me that authentic healing sometimes begins by loudly asserting "stop" when a boundary is crossed. The lesson in meeting a problematic practitioner could be in discovering the power of saying "no." This isn't to suggest seeking out negative experiences, but to recognize that there is value in walking away and choosing not to engage further with someone who doesn't respect your boundaries.

Transformation is a deeply personal process that adheres to no one else's timeline but your own. You have autonomy over your body and the right to set your limits. If you find yourself in a group where conformity is the norm, resist the urge to follow if it crosses your comfort zone. Your healing may well involve ignoring others' judgments and voicing your true feelings, even at the risk of discomfort. Saying "no" with confidence and assertion may be a significant step in your healing journey—it's your body, your space, and your rules.

10. Illuminated Paths: Steering Through the Continuum of Self-Healing

A Closer Look at Intimate Relationships Between Healer and Client

Sometimes, our relationships with coaches, therapists, or practitioners can feel more intimate than relationships with our spouses, friends, or family. If we feel completely comfortable being authentic and vulnerable, the bond naturally strengthens. This is particularly true if the practitioner validates us, aids our growth, illuminates areas needing improvement, disagrees with our negative self-talk, and helps us feel our own love and essence.

Feeling better about ourselves inevitably brings out our own inner love. When our hearts open, possibly for the first time in a long time, we might naturally assume it's due to an attraction to the practitioner. We could misinterpret this as chemistry, projecting romantic feelings onto the coach, healer, or therapist. It's crucial that you feel at ease to share what's surfacing for you during your healing process, even if it's embarrassing or uncomfortable. A practitioner should establish safe boundaries and an environment where transparency is encouraged with all your thoughts and feelings, including sexual or intimate ones.

If you are uncomfortable being transparent with the practitioner about the thoughts, fantasies, or feelings arising within the client-practitioner relationship, this could impede the healing process. This isn't because you have these feelings, but because you cannot be authentic by repressing emotions. It may indicate that the practitioner is not a suitable fit for you, and that is acceptable. In such instances, it might be better to consider working with someone else. Conversely, if you are working with a practitioner who upholds firm boundaries and fosters transparent communication, trust can be built.

Being able to share your most intimate thoughts, fantasies, and wild imagination can make the therapeutic conversations and the relationship itself incredibly powerful for your healing. This is because a good practitioner acts as a benign observer or sounding board,

10. Illuminated Paths: Steering Through the Continuum of Self-Healing

essentially helping you to hear your own words as though they were reflected back at you by a nonjudgmental mirror. This allows you to compassionately witness and hear your unconscious fears, stories, and beliefs.

It's becoming more common for therapists and coaches to share their opinions, insights, and personal experiences if they believe it will benefit the client. Many clients favor this interactive approach over one where they're doing all the talking, with the practitioner offering minimal contributions, solutions, or tools. However, those who prefer traditional therapy and are used to doing all the talking often do not find a good fit with me because they do not want me to share my stories, even when they're highly relevant to their issues.

There could also be a risk associated with developing an open, transparent emotional dialogue with a healing practitioner or coach. This could lead to the practitioner becoming biased or emotionally triggered by what the client shares. The challenge here is maintaining detachment from the client's story if the practitioner develops genuine empathy or deep feelings for the client. While it might initially feel good to know our practitioner genuinely cares about us, complications could arise. They may start responding to our stories, feelings, and beliefs in ways similar to our friends or family. You might sense them taking things personally and struggling to remain neutral and objective. Their advice or opinions may begin to reflect their own experiences and perspectives, rather than providing the insightful and helpful guidance we expect in a safe coaching or healing environment.

If this occurs, we may start to feel uneasy about being open and sharing our deepest thoughts and experiences. As a result, our relationship with the practitioner may echo past dynamics with parents or partners where emotional support was lacking in compassion. We're aware of instances where clients form intimate bonds with their therapists or coaches. Some practitioners, especially within

10. Illuminated Paths: Steering Through the Continuum of Self-Healing

tantric circles, endorse this, claiming it furthers personal growth and shadow integration. However, it often leads to disastrous outcomes and complicates the healing process.

Inappropriate boundaries can introduce new issues and may even exacerbate trauma, particularly when a practitioner assumes a parental figure for a client who is recovering from past abuse by a family member or authority figure.

Should the client-practitioner relationship end abruptly, leaving the client feeling rejected, confused, or retraumatized, the psychological and emotional fallout could be profound. It may intensify feelings of distrust, solidifying beliefs that they are beyond help, that others are merely seeking sexual connections, or are manipulative, echoing their childhood experiences. This could deeply undermine their confidence in the healing process. If the client then seeks a new path and practitioner, they may face the added challenge of healing from the trauma incurred with the previous coach or therapist, while still dealing with their initial childhood wounds. Ultimately, they might require therapy to resolve both the issues from their past and the distress or boundary violations inflicted by their former therapist or coach.

I strongly recommend that clients avoid practitioners who lack training and experience in treating those with trauma histories. It's equally vital to engage with a practitioner who can relate to your background, appreciating the influences of your culture, generational context, and the collective narratives that have shaped you. For instance, guru-disciple dynamics rooted in Eastern traditions were historically beneficial in societies that valued and cultivated spiritual growth and learning. Yet, the principles from these traditions may not align with the complexities of contemporary life. A practitioner from an Eastern background may not fully grasp the nuanced emotional and relational issues prevalent in the West, such as body dysmorphia, the tension between individualism and collectivism, or differing communication styles. Consequently, those deeply versed in Eastern philosophies may struggle to connect with or comprehend the particular challenges faced by Western individuals. For example, seeking parenting advice might not be ideal from a practitioner without personal experience in raising children.

Expressing yourself and setting boundaries is essential, even if it means ending a relationship. If the dynamic is healthy for you, you may choose to continue. But if it's not working, you have the right to walk away. On the other hand, if the practitioner is understanding, maintains healthy boundaries, and communicates effectively, it might be beneficial to stay, even if it's uncomfortable. This could teach you valuable skills in communication, conflict management, and emotional regulation, which can enhance your future relationships.

The Misunderstanding of Tantra and Sexuality

There are numerous practices that may lead to confusion, harm, and boundary crossings. However, I want to particularly draw attention to Neo-Tantra. In most instances I've encountered, clients participating in these practices end up more traumatized. They often become entangled in unhealthy sexual relationships with practitioners and are persuaded to engage in group activities. These could include sensual touch, nude dancing, sensual massages, or even engaging in sexual activities to improve their sex lives and enhance their relationships.

One of the primary reasons for re-traumatization, manipulation, and boundary breaches is that many individuals who become sex educators and facilitators have themselves experienced sexual trauma. While they might adopt a sex-positive approach to sexuality, which some find refreshing, their attempts to challenge sexual taboos can be seen as empowering. They might communicate more explicitly and dress provocatively, aiming to normalize sexuality. Their discourse

10. Illuminated Paths: Steering Through the Continuum of Self-Healing

may be laden with complex medical terminology, in an effort to appear knowledgeable and professional within the sphere of sexuality. However, their behavior and the maintenance of professional boundaries could be inconsistent, potentially leading to further confusion or trauma for those who have previously experienced sexual abuse.

Sexuality often remains a deeply hidden and uncomfortable subject for many, heavily shaped by personal beliefs formed during upbringing. The views of sex educators or tantra teachers may greatly differ from those taught by parents or ingrained by culture. With these conflicting perspectives on sexuality, it can be especially confusing and overwhelming for those who have internalized guilt and shame about their sexual identity. Since sexuality is intertwined with our fundamental existence and survival, our natural essence cannot be ignored. It embodies our core nature: to bond, experience pleasure, procreate, and feel attraction. It connects us to our masculinity or femininity and can foster a sense of belonging within our gender group.

Without a clear understanding of what constitutes a healthy sexual relationship with ourselves or our partners, it can be difficult to discern what is healthy and what is not, to find appropriate role models, practitioners, or teachers, or to know which sexual healing practices may be beneficial for us. To complicate this further, since the topic of sexuality often remains in the shadows collectively, it can be challenging to know whom to discuss it with or where to seek help when needed, or to share our hidden beliefs and fantasies.

Physical touch and sex, which release feel-good chemicals in our bodies and create pleasure, can often be misinterpreted as healing because *we feel good*. However, this pleasure can be misleading and should not be used as a reliable measure of the effectiveness of tantric practices in resolving issues around sexuality. For those struggling with guilt and shame around sexuality, there can be a significant

10. Illuminated Paths: Steering Through the Continuum of Self-Healing

cathartic release through experiencing both pain and pleasure, which may be perceived as beneficial for healing. However, there is the risk of a dopamine crash after such experiences, and without healthy boundaries, integration, and new positive actions, a client may feel violated and more vulnerable afterward. This is particularly true if they have engaged in any form of intimacy with the practitioner or other participants.

I recommend that individuals with a history of sexual trauma work with a practitioner of the same gender, consider attending healing sessions with a trusted friend, or initially seek guidance from a practitioner specialized in somatic experience work. This is especially crucial if you're considering healing modalities involving physical touch. Consulting with a licensed therapist to establish clear personal boundaries before engaging in tantric work can also be advantageous. Remember, it's your body and your rules! For those who recognize their blockages and wish to open up gradually, starting with professional massage at a reputable facility with positive reviews or referrals may provide a safe way to experience non-threatening physical touch.

Understanding Plant Medicine

Plant medicines like ayahuasca, kambo, cannabis, and psilocybin are gaining traction in Western culture, with research increasingly supporting their efficacy in therapeutic settings. For instance, controlled studies have combined psilocybin with psychotherapy to help those with PTSD.

Yet, for individuals with unresolved traumas such as sexual abuse, or struggles with substance misuse, plant medicine may pose risks, potentially leading to destabilization during or after a ceremony. While spiritual growth and self-discovery are significant, the practicalities of life cannot be overlooked. Stability and a grounded approach are necessary to process and integrate these experiences effectively.

10. Illuminated Paths: Steering Through the Continuum of Self-Healing

The current lack of regulation in plant medicine ceremonies, including the certification of practitioners, raises concerns. Essential safety procedures, like mental health screenings and aftercare support, are often not uniformly applied. Ideally, ceremonies should be complemented with follow-up sessions for ongoing support and coaching. In the absence of these safeguards, participants may re-enter their daily routines, such as getting the kids ready for school, responding to early morning business emails, or just feeling clear, with difficulty.

Plant medicines, long utilized in indigenous cultures, pose unique challenges when integrated into Western settings. These substances were traditionally used in contexts with different lifestyles, support structures, and knowledge systems. Westerners could feel overwhelmed without adequate time and support for decompression and integration, struggling to integrate profound insights into their personal and professional lives. They could struggle with a newfound awareness of dissatisfaction in their careers, financial limitations, or the realization of toxic relationships coupled with familial commitments. Without proper integration support, these intense experiences can become overwhelming and confusing.

Furthermore, advice from modern-day shamans and practitioners might not always resonate, especially if they do not comprehend daily responsibilities such as childcare. These practitioners may dismiss post-ceremony confusion as a normal part of the process and might encourage participants to let go of what they consider false identities. Instead of promoting the integration of insights and their practical application through coaching, some practitioners might propose more plant medicine sessions and ceremonies. This approach risks leading to a cycle of perpetual processing without meaningful, positive changes in one's relationships, healing from past trauma, or personal empowerment.

10. Illuminated Paths: Steering Through the Continuum of Self-Healing

The sense of unity in a sacred circle may foster a false sense of progress. Euphoric sensations and the resulting neurochemical changes could mislead participants into believing they are on a transformative path. However, the optimism felt during ceremonies and the new positive narratives spun around plant medicine journeys can be misleading if there's no tangible progress in mending relationships, sorting out finances, or enhancing communication. Without these changes, one's life, health, and interpersonal connections might not improve. Therefore, it's essential to approach plant medicine circles with discernment, valuing their ability to expand consciousness while understanding they're not a cure-all. Real growth requires action upon newfound insights. It's also important to confront our issues when not under the influence of plant substances, to trust our judgment, maintain our routines, and take breaks from various practices when necessary. This ensures our insights are not just theoretical but are integrated and enacted in substantial and beneficial ways in our daily lives.

Dodging the Workshop Junkie Lifestyle and Cult-Like Healing Communities

As you navigate your healing journey, you may meet people eager to share and even push their transformative experiences with workshops and events onto you, whether you've sought their advice or not. Even when you express satisfaction with your progress, they may view you through their perspective, assuming you need the same transformation they experienced. This insistence could be driven by their desire to spread the word or perhaps a motive like earning a commission for referrals. These individuals may not be aware of your trauma history, current therapeutic work, or specific sensitivities. You may already be well on your path to recovery, finding that their suggestions don't align with your needs. Conversely, as a newcomer to healing, you might feel

10. Illuminated Paths: Steering Through the Continuum of Self-Healing

overwhelmed or pressured, needing time to understand your needs before engaging with larger groups.

Healing communities often foster a sense of kinship, a comfort particularly during shadow work and when healing from toxic relationships or difficult family histories. However, their persistence in keeping you coming back can sometimes seem overbearing or even cult-like. Healing is a personal journey, not a straight line, and it progresses at your own pace. Many self-improvement programs, despite their compelling titles and unique descriptions, are reiterations of older teachings. Instructors often adapt what they've learned from their mentors, infusing it with their own personality, cultural lens, and interpretation. Frequently, they offer common transformative tools, repackaged with different names, or combined into new methods to suit a contemporary outlook.

Every community and culture harbors *hidden beliefs and shadows*, despite good intentions. This is often because facilitators, despite being well-intentioned, may not have confronted their own *shadow work*—the unaddressed personal issues and unhealed aspects of themselves. Such unresolved issues can lead to dogmatism, arrogance, and an obsessive or self-righteous demeanor. Consequently, even the most profound life philosophies and tools can be tainted by unhealed trauma within their consciousness. As a result, they may misuse these tools or misinterpret philosophies, projecting their unexamined ego onto your healing path, or display communication that feels judgmental and pressuring.

We've all seen individuals who, upon overcoming alcoholism, become fixated on the perceived drinking problems of others. Their addictive tendencies might shift from alcohol to smoking or excessive coffee drinking. Later, they might embrace a new identity, like becoming a born-again Christian, and start proselytizing with the same fervor previously directed at sobriety. To friends, family, or coworkers, their

10. Illuminated Paths: Steering Through the Continuum of Self-Healing

intense, addictive personality remains unchanged—it is the substance or doctrine that has shifted. Even though they are now sober and devout Christians, they appear ungrounded and overly confident in their newfound *answers*, eager to *save* others without having truly uncovered the roots of their narcissistic, pushy personality.

Your self-improvement and healing path is uniquely yours. It's essential to ensure that any retreat, seminar, or instructor you choose aligns with your lifestyle and values. Despite the accolades a program or practitioner might receive, verify the consistency between their words and their actions. Look beyond the promotional language and evaluate the outcomes: Are their students living the improved life they seek? Notice if the clients are genuinely happier, have overcome their fear of flying, or are venturing into dating after a divorce. It's not enough to simply feel good or become enamored with new spiritual teachings and life tools; you should look for real, positive progress in your life. Remember, you are the best judge of what suits your healing journey. If you feel the need to take a break, honor that. Always prioritize your best interest.

Men's and Women's Work: Is it Relevant or Gender Fluid for Our Collective Expansion

Support groups are forming to tackle gender-specific issues, such as the impacts of restrictive masculinity or femininity. These groups strive to foster a space where individuals can freely express their gender, providing a supportive environment for discussions on topics like dating, sexual abuse, and bisexual curiosity, or concerns about feeling inadequately masculine or feminine, attractiveness in aging, and navigating life transitions such as hormonal changes and motherhood.

Such groups could serve as sanctuaries for shedding societal expectations, pushing personal boundaries, and gaining confidence.

10. Illuminated Paths: Steering Through the Continuum of Self-Healing

They challenge traditional gender roles, encouraging a broader acceptance of one's identity. Furthermore, they empower individuals, aiding women in gaining independence or leaving toxic relationships, and assisting men in openly expressing their emotions. As perceptions of gender evolve, acknowledging this diversity becomes increasingly crucial.

Some groups may cling to outdated notions like those from the 1950s regarding gender roles. Facilitators could also introduce their own biases, potentially leading to derogatory remarks about women or men. There's a risk of advice rooted in fear or unresolved trauma, such as making broad, negative generalizations based on personal adverse experiences.

As society moves towards more fluid gender expression, it's important to be discerning of biases within these groups. Recognize that some teachings may be archaic and not reflect the current understanding of gender. It's essential to trust your own judgment and honor the uniqueness of your journey in understanding and expressing your gender identity. The more a group or teacher insists on polarized views, the less it may resonate with you if your aim is to find peace with your gender expression, to approach others' expressions with compassion, and to reject beliefs that do not resonate with your authentic self.

I've put together a set of eleven simple questions to help you evaluate a practitioner or program. Use this list to identify potential issues and check if they align with your values and goals:

1. Is the teacher exemplifying the lessons they are teaching?
2. Do the values conveyed in the teachings align with mine?
3. Could there be potential harm to myself or others through engagement in this method?
4. Am I genuinely at ease with declining this program or session if I don't like it?

10. Illuminated Paths: Steering Through the Continuum of Self-Healing

5. Are they requesting a commitment I'm not prepared to give?
6. Am I comfortable with discontinuing if I don't perceive any benefits?
7. Are there additional proofs, references, or testimonials that could validate this teacher or program?
8. How open and responsive are the teacher and program to my queries?
9. Is the communication clear, open, and cooperative, so I feel seen and heard for who I am?
10. Do graduates from the program seem content and have achieved the positive results I'm aiming for?
11. Am I undertaking this truly for myself or on behalf of someone else?

11
Beyond the Matrix: The Emergence of the Heart-Centered Human

This book delves into uncovering hidden beliefs, understanding our archetypal shadows, and smoothing out personality friction points, leading us towards a healthier personal evolution and improved relationships. But what could we become when we transcend our old mental programming? How does our purpose transform, and what new meanings do we discover in life when we awaken from the matrix and realize, with renewed self-awareness, that life offers more than what we've been conditioned to believe?

Imagine a life in which we fully embrace our authentic masculine and feminine energies, connect with our emotions without reactivity, uphold healthy boundaries, and take actions that better our lives while contributing to humanity's welfare. Envision a society where everyone strives for common ground, bringing forth their best through integrity, impeccable communication, commendable work ethics, and positivity.

In this new version of Earth, how would we, as evolved beings, present ourselves? What beliefs would guide our actions and purpose? Within a thriving society, what collective expectations would its citizens uphold? Instead of awaiting a savior, we would step up, embracing personal accountability, pursuing self-improvement, offering forgiveness readily, and committing to being good humans for harmonious coexistence. If anyone strayed from our shared vision of compassion and harmony, it would stand out, and course correction would arise from personal responsibility, as the majority would live with open hearts, striving for peace, love, and success for all.

I envision this world already and have chosen to embody heaven on earth, establishing my own principles—my creed, my philosophy, which I call "The Tao of the Heart-Centered Human." These twenty-six attributes are distilled from the finest traits I've observed in my parents, successful entrepreneurs, esteemed mentors, and individuals who navigate life's challenges with grace. My aim is not to dictate a universal blueprint for human behavior, nor to claim that my approach is the pinnacle of perfection or harmony. Yet, in my experience, those I admire consistently take the higher road, choose love over fear, stay true to their soul's journey, lead with their hearts, and contribute tirelessly to a confident, thriving society.

The Tao of the Heart-Centered Human

- Put your integrity into everything you do.
- If you feel fear, work through it.
- Hold no one responsible for your pain.
- Approach every life situation as if it's a piece of art, and you are the painter.

11. Beyond the Matrix: The Emergence of the Heart-Centered Human

- You teach people how to treat you.
- Excuses are merely beliefs, and they remain your responsibility.
- Remain authentic, even if it means facing disapproval from others.
- Don't consent to things that you believe are harmful to you or others.
- If something isn't working, employ creativity until it does.
- Learn to let go of things that are meant to end or change so that you too can grow and expand.
- Change is inevitable, and when you embrace it, resistance ceases and miracles occur.
- Confront challenges head-on.
- Choose to face the challenge rather than settling into complacency.
- Happiness is a present reality, and it's your choice to ease into it.
- Saying "no" and establishing boundaries equates to saying "yes" to your authentic self.
- Blaming prevents you from taking responsibility for creating what you desire.
- Admit when you make a mistake, for you're learning about life every day.
- Asking for help provides another person with a purposeful opportunity to assist you.
- Never settle for less than what you're worth.
- Even when you're angry, let love prevail.
- Your spiritual practice should involve finding lightness even when facing challenges.
- Commit to following through on your promises or be ready to accept the consequences.

11. Beyond the Matrix: The Emergence of the Heart-Centered Human

- If someone confides in you, cherish their trust.
- Learn to find comfort amidst discomfort.
- Keep learning—you can never know too much.
- Define yourself not by your past, but by who you choose to be today.
- Since you're constantly learning about life, feelings of guilt or regret are choices.
- Every day, you embody the miraculous essence of life.
- Balance in life is achieved through giving and receiving.
- Avoid taking yourself or life too seriously; after all, change is the only constant.
- Remember, you are solely responsible for your emotions.
- People will judge you more by your actions than by your words.
- Opinions about you are usually based on how you make people feel, rather than what you say.

One might wonder, "What would two heart-centered individuals be like in an intimate romantic relationship, business partnership, or friendship?" If they were to embody the twenty-six traits I've delineated, how would they communicate and interact with each other and navigate the dynamics of their relationships?

To foster an authentic, empowered relationship, being present and centered in the heart is essential. As we let go of our outdated stories and step into our genuine, vibrational essence, our communication deepens and expands. This is because both individuals cultivate a healthy connection with a higher power—be it God, Spirit, or Source—before anything else. Their physical relationships then become a strong, sustainable extension of this divine connection. Such alignment with our soul and spirit paves the way for what I term an *empowered relationship*. This concept goes beyond the bond between individuals,

11. Beyond the Matrix: The Emergence of the Heart-Centered Human

introducing a third dimension to the relationship, similar to a person's connection with the Holy Spirit or God, although not necessarily tied to religion.

Connecting to the divine or a higher power, the empowered relationship transcends its individual members, affecting not just couples, business partners, or friends but also families, communities, and the collective consciousness. The growth and presence of each person have a broader impact. Thus, the relationship becomes its own force, with its unique dynamics. When two people engage with love and compassion, their positive influence extends even to onlookers. Every relationship creates ripples; these ripples, born from the relationship's own energy, have the potential to uplift those around them.

In such authentic and empowered relationships, real magic unfolds, and more positive synchronicities appear, as if the universe conspires for our well-being. This defines what I call an authentic *power couple*, relevant to both lovers and close friends. By revealing each other's hidden beliefs and shadows, we energize and actualize our true potential.

The empowered relationship fosters a deep connection with our emotional selves, our unique essence, and our existence. It involves forming a conscious partnership with oneself and the world. Every interaction, whether fleeting or long-lasting, is a sacred space. Self-improvement reflects the broader universe. In this dynamic, blame, victimhood, and superficial reasons for problems are addressed with accountability, curiosity, and communication from a self-reflective stance. This requires consistently embracing our vulnerabilities and shadows with compassion and acknowledging our participation in situations.

When healing ourselves and undergoing our own transformation, relationships and communication may evolve through four stages of belief systems to reach an empowered state, moving beyond blame, survival instincts, jealousy, and insecurities. This evolution enables individuals to overcome persistent negative patterns, such as constant arguments over finances or feelings of inadequacy, and to take personal responsibility.

Here's a simplified breakdown of the belief systems:

Disempowered Belief System:

"You make me so mad."

"The world is unsafe."

"You stress me out."

Apparent Belief System:

"I get mad when you point out what's wrong."

"I don't feel safe going out alone since I was mugged."

"I am stressed because of my excessive workload."

Authentic Belief System:

"I feel incompetent."

"I doubt my decisions."

"I'm afraid to tell my boss she's overloading me."

Empowered Belief System:

"I do my best and improve as I learn."

"I trust my heart and manage my life well, regardless of changes."

"I speak my truth, trusting that others will align with me or not, and I am content with either."

In the empowered belief system, individuals transcend past narratives, connecting like the purity seen in a child's eyes allows one to glimpse another's soul. Interactions become co-creative, driven by love and growth, free from history's weight, cultural constraints,

11. Beyond the Matrix: The Emergence of the Heart-Centered Human

and trauma responses. They open to the greatest possibilities for excitement and rejuvenation in relationships.

In this spiritually empowered relationship container, we may give each other permission to call out when we're playing small, seeming depressed, or communicating in a stressed, angry manner. This isn't to criticize negatively but to invite a return to one's best self. Such relationships avoid stagnation, hidden regressions, or resentment. There's no need for walking on eggshells; instead, we maintain a space free from negative emotional narratives.

True, transparent, and authentic connections might push some away, especially those we can't relate to or with whom we've been inauthentic to avoid conflict. If someone becomes defensive when you share emotions or point out hurtful behaviors, they may lack awareness or the consciousness to see things from a heart-centered perspective. Offering them this book is an option, though their reaction may vary, and their boundaries should be respected.

I have many acquaintances, from high school friends to bandmates; these connections are light yet heartfelt. In my closer spiritual community, we share language and visions for health and a sustainable Earth. This doesn't mean we're without friction or that everyone has done the necessary shadow work to engage deeply and handle feedback.

But there are some friends with whom we can discuss everything. We can get triggered and share in real time what comes up, taking personal responsibility. There doesn't need to be such seriousness and weight in misunderstandings. There's a reverence for each other without attachment to the outcome. These relationships are what hold my life together. Even if only ten percent of my friends—say, out of one hundred people I know—belong to this category; these thriving, conscious relationships shape my daily reality, which is filled with love, excitement, hope, and trust in humanity.

I'm creating a community of friends and people who take personal

11. Beyond the Matrix: The Emergence of the Heart-Centered Human

responsibility, and I would love for you to join us. This group isn't for the elite but for open-hearted individuals who are driven to create a better Earth and culture. It's for those who practice what they preach and for those who understand that the younger generations are watching and want to model the happy, sustainable world in which they wish to live.

So, how do you take massive action now? You might feel that you need more support beyond the exercises in this book. I want to help you reach heights of success in your relationships and life beyond what you could have ever imagined. My coaching programs offer the steps to catapult you over any barriers that have been in your way. The extraordinary life you've dreamed of exists—I've seen it!

Many people will read this book and perhaps never engage with the exercises, or if they do, they might approach them in a logical and rushed manner, thus missing out on the true benefits. Others may require a life map and additional guidance to direct them towards actionable steps, which is what I have provided. Whether you're a single working mother with very little time, a businessman who works long hours, someone without the financial resources to attend a retreat, or if you live in a country with limited resources, or face any other challenges, I've made it simple for you to stay connected to your transformation.

Visit raydoktor.com/tools to access the membership area and download "The Tao of the Heart-Centered Human" for daily inspiration. Place it where you'll see it often, to serve as a constant guide. Support is easy to find. Within the membership area, join a community, receive consistent, uplifting life tools, and keep informed about all my workshops and online events.

I want to express my deep gratitude for the time you've spent with me and for the trust you've placed in choosing this book. The connection and kinship we've formed through these pages are precious to me, whether or not we meet in person. Your willingness to view life through a new, conscious lens and to allow me to guide you is a gift—a testament to the emerging, improved version of yourself. Every small step you take is a leap towards the life you desire.

With all my heart, I appreciate your commitment to growth. You are not alone on this path. Should you ever feel stuck, need a reminder, or simply seek the warmth of positive support, this book will always be here for you. Until we meet again, whether in these pages or perhaps in another space of learning and growth, I'll be looking forward to seeing the wonders you will discover on your journey.

With deep gratitude and appreciation,
Ray Doktor, Psy. D.

11. Beyond the Matrix: The Emergence of the Heart-Centered Human

About Ray Doktor

Ray Doktor, Psy. D., is a seasoned life and relationship coach with three decades of experience, guiding over 6,000 clients to overcome limiting beliefs and navigate life's challenges. His work has empowered many to build greater confidence, trust in themselves, and achieve happiness, resulting in thriving individuals and families.

He holds a doctoral degree in clinical psychology, a master's degree in counseling psychology, and a bachelor's degree in human behavior. His extensive toolkit includes hypnotherapy, guided imagery, EMDR, NLP, qigong, PSYCH-K, meditation, yoga, sound healing, somatic experience, and shamanic training. Dr. Ray is a true alchemist, integrating psychology with the wisdom of Eastern philosophies, modern science, and spirituality.

In addition to his professional pursuits, he is a father, musician, workshop facilitator, gardener, and athlete who revels in adventure and the great outdoors. Dr. Ray resides in Ashland, Oregon, in the United States. And yes, "Doktor" is indeed his real surname—which he finds amusing, and you're welcome to share a laugh with him about it!

Unlock Your Potential and Stay Connected: A Personal Invitation from Ray Doktor, Psy. D.

Dive Deeper and Connect with an Arsenal of Tools and Inspiration

As we turn the final page of "All It Takes is One," the invitation to continue this transformative journey doesn't end here. Whether you're seeking further guidance, tools to deepen your practice, or simply wish to stay connected and inspired, I invite you to join me beyond the pages of this book.

Access Free Tools and Resources for This Book

Dive into a curated collection of resources designed to complement your journey of self-discovery and mastery. From insightful exercises to practical guides, everything you need to continue your path of growth awaits. Visit https://raydoktor.com/tools/ to unlock these free tools and begin exploring.

Stay Connected With Me

The conversation and connection don't have to end here. Join me on my website and social media platforms, where the dialogue on self-mastery, growth, and healing continues. Let's journey together, share insights, and foster a community of like-minded individuals dedicated to personal evolution.

- **Website: raydoktor.com/**
- **Facebook: facebook.com/raydoktor**
- **Instagram: instagram.com/raydoktor/**
- **TikTok: tiktok.com/@raydoktor**
- **YouTube: youtube.com/@raydoktor**

Your journey of self-discovery and mastery is uniquely yours, but you don't have to walk it alone. Connect, explore, and continue to grow. Let's unlock your fullest potential together.

www.ingramcontent.com/pod-product-compliance
Lightning Source LLC
Chambersburg PA
CBHW070151100426
42743CB00013B/2874